PLANNERS AND PLANES:

AIRPORTS AND LAND-USE COMPATIBILITY

Susan M. Schalk, AICP, WITH STEPHANIE A. D. WARD, AICP

TABLE OF CONTENTS

Contributors

Rick Busch serves as the director of planning for Denver International Airport and is responsible for the airport's planning and noise activities. He has spent 25 years working at large hub airports and another 11 years as an airport and noise and land-use consultant. Busch and his staff at DIA won the 2010 AIAA/AAAE/ACC Jay Hollingsworth Speas Award for noise mitigation and land-use control efforts.

Tait Galloway serves as senior airport and transportation planner for the City of San Diego.

Alex Iams is a commercial development planner with Arlington Economic Development, a department of the Arlington County government. His work supports various components of the county sector-planning process, including how proposed buildings would relate to operations at Ronald Reagan Washington National Airport.

Mark R. Johnson, AICP, is a director of Ricondo & Associates, an aviation consultancy headquartered in Chicago, where he serves as the technical services coordinator for land use. He has extensive experience in airport noise and land-use compatibility planning, having managed the preparation of 30 Part 150 Noise Compatibility Programs and 25 airport land-use compatibility plans. He has consulted with the California Energy Commission in assessing the airport compatibility implications of proposed power plants and served on the advisory panel for the Airport Cooperative Research Program project, Enhancing Airport Land Use Compatibility Planning.

Robert A. Leiter, FAICP, served as director of land use and transportation planning for the San Diego Association of Governments (SANDAG) from 2003 to 2009. He now serves as a consultant to SANDAG on SB-375 implementation.

Carol A. Lurie, AICP—a principal at VHB/Vanasse Hangen Brustlin, a transportation, planning, and environmental consulting firm—is an expert manager of large complex environmental-impact statements and airport sustainability projects. She prepared the award-winning San Francisco Airport Sustainability Report, the Logan Airport Annual Environmental Report, and the Philadelphia Airport Stewardship Plan, and she is working on the Ithaca Tompkins Regional Airport Sustainable Master Plan and the Environmental Management Plan for the Northeastern Florida Regional Airport at St. Augustine, Florida.

Maria J. Muia is a private pilot with SEL-I, AGI, IGI, and an SME Green Specialist Certificate from Purdue University. She has more than 20 years of aviation industry experience in both the public and private sectors in aviation planning, facility requirements, operations, activity forecasting, environmental issues, government agency coordination, research, and project funding.

Linda Perry is a director with LeighFisher, specializing in economic analyses, aviation demand forecasting, and comparative evaluations of airline service, route networks, and airfares. She has more than 20 years of experience and is the leader of Leigh Fisher's forecasting and economics practice.

David B. Rickerson is a senior director with the firm of Planning Technology. He began his career as a public-sector land-use planner focusing on growth management planning and the administration and implementation of zoning codes. For the past 26 years, Rickerson has specialized in airport master planning, collateral development planning, and aviation facility development and land-use compatibility planning for airports throughout the United States and internationally.

John van Woensel leads CH2M HILL's national airport-planning practice and has 25 years of experience in airport planning and environmental planning for airports of all sizes. He has led or participated in airport planning and environmental planning assignments from Alaska to Montana and Florida. Airport clients have included Pittsburgh, Cincinnati/Northern Kentucky, Palm Beach, Baltimore Washington, Hartsfield-Jackson, and Philadelphia International airports. John is a private pilot and also works for numerous smaller general-aviation airports.

Keith Wilschetz serves as director of planning for the San Diego County Regional Airport Authority.

Holland Young leads the master planning practice for LeighFisher and has 30 years of aviation experience. His experience includes airport master plans, sustainability plans, site selection studies, commercial development plans, environmental assessments and impact statements, and air service analyses. As the former planning and environmental manager for the development of Austin-Bergstrom International Airport, Young was responsible for all planning and environmental efforts in the conversion of the former Air Force base into a replacement commercial-service airport for the central Texas region.

CHAPTER 1

Linking Airport Planning
to Community Planning

Susan M. Schalk, AICP

Links between community planning and airport planning are necessary and often overlooked. If an airport is to be fully useful and effective, it must be carefully and regularly considered in the community planning process; conversely, airport planning must understand and consider the needs and concerns of the communities that surround, abut, and make use of the airport.

1

Successful public airports are supported by a range of airport planning activities and processes. It is common for community planners to incorporate an existing airport master plan and its findings into the community's comprehensive plan. Or, upon the completion of an airport master plan, the airport sponsor may turn to community planners to implement compatible land-use ordinances and regulations that support the airport vision.

The premise of this PAS Report is that neither of these approaches is truly successful unless airport planners and community planners work as partners during the development of planning processes in order to weave the community vision, strategies, and values together with those embedded in airport planning. The next four chapters identify and provide examples of ways in which community planners can become more productively engaged in the airport planning process.

Because there are very few planning processes under way at this time that address new airports, this report focuses on the preparation of airport master plan updates and the engagement of community planners during the update process in order to incorporate their unique knowledge about the communities served by the airport. An airport master plan (and its update) is a comprehensive study of an airport that usually describes short-, medium-, and long-term development plans to meet anticipated future aviation demand. The master plan updates discussed in this report have been developed for airports of all sizes: from large commercial-service airports located in urban areas to small general-aviation airports located in rural areas. Master plan updates can therefore vary in level of detail and associated effort. The elements of a master planning process will also vary in complexity and level of detail, depending on the size, function, issues, and problems of the individual airport. As a result, study elements for large or complex airports may involve unique technical analyses.[1]

For the most part, the quality of the intersection between airport planning and community planning is evident in the compatibility of the airport's surrounding land uses. The Federal Aviation Administration (FAA) has recently sponsored an extensive research project through the Airport Comprehensive Research Program (ACRP) on land-use fundamentals. In short, the ACRP guide provides a "comprehensive resource of information and recommendations that can be used to address land use compatibility issues and protect the viability of every airport."[2] This PAS Report is a companion piece to the ACRP research on measures to enhance land-use compatibility, focusing on the airport master planning process and opportunities for community planners to become engaged in the airport planning processes early enough to allow for stronger links and improved results.

An airport master plan puts forward recommendations for the safe, efficient, and economical development of an airport in order to meet the needs of the communities it serves. The plan should be thoughtful, well-coordinated, practical, and cost-effective; include a realistic assessment of needs and resources; and be consistent with established goals and objectives. The master planning process considers safety first, along with capacity considerations when planning for the future. In addition, the plan should consider future enhancements planned by the FAA due to advances in technology.[3]

Planning programs for public airports are typically sponsored by a public agency, usually the owner and operator of the airport. The airport's sponsor may or may not be represented by the same policy makers as the communities surrounding the airport, and these actors may or may not be responsible for the comprehensive plan for the airport's community and region.

Although the development or updating of an airport master plan is usually the initial step in the airport planning process, airport planning extends beyond that document to also encompass metropolitan airport system planning, state airport system planning, and the National Plan of Integrated Airport Systems (NPIAS), which is administered by the FAA. In fact, the FAA is particularly interested in systematic airport planning that considers the national system plan, to ensure "the effective use of airport resources in order to satisfy aviation demand in a financially feasible manner."[4] The community planner's perspective, in contrast, will usually be driven instead by local conditions. Since the airport's sponsor may be pulled in two directions—to respond to the larger demands of the national system or to respond to local planning challenges, which may or may not be in conflict with the national-scale objectives—early partnerships and collective planning efforts become essential.

The typical airport master plan update, which presents the airport's comprehensive vision for development over 20 years or longer, includes:

- An inventory of the existing airport facilities and graphic representations of both the existing and the anticipated airport development and land use

- A delineation of the role of the airport in the local, regional, and national aviation systems

- A definition of the current aviation demand at the airport and a projection of future demand

- A technical and procedural assessment of the demand that lays out various options for growth and offers data on their projected cost-effectiveness

- A financial plan to support development

- A framework for a continuous planning process, which is triggered by one of three motives:

  - the completion of development programs, leaving in question future needs

  - a desire to update or refine the vision for the future

  - the FAA's request for further planning to investigate the eligibility of federal funding for proposed developments

In addition to providing a systematic process for determining what facilities will be needed to satisfy anticipated aviation demand, the preparation of an airport master plan is a mechanism for determining whether any or the proposed development is eligible for federal funding. Airport funding is contingent upon the FAA's approval of certain components of the airport planning process, including the forecasts, selection of the most demanding aircraft users (referred to as critical aircraft) to define the airport's design criteria, and airport layout plan. The FAA has provided particular guidance for airport master plans and airport design criteria through advisory circulars that it distributes.[5]

Key to airport planning efforts is an extensive public outreach process to consider community opinions during the articulation of goals relative to the airport and its future development. The best ways for the community planner to become engaged in the airport planning process include:

- Participating as a critical stakeholder in the development of a vision for the airport's future, ensuring strong links between the community's economic strategy and the airport's long-term vision. (See Chapter 2.)

- Supporting preparation of aviation forecasts by providing local knowledge and research about socioeconomic factors in the airport's market area, with continued involvement in facility requirements, alternatives analysis, and financial strategies. (See Chapter 3.)

- Integrating compatible land-use planning that links the airport master plan with the comprehensive plan for the municipality or region. (See Chapter 4.)

THE RELATIONSHIP BETWEEN AIRPORT AND COMMUNITY PLANNING TECHNIQUES

Stephanie A. D. Ward, AICP

Planning for the development of compatible land uses near airports is a complicated process due to the number of agencies involved in the planning process and the methods of implementation for various land-use controls. The relationship between an airport's operations and community planning techniques create a complex web of potential interactions. (See Figure 1.1.) Community planners need to be involved in the master planning efforts to ensure that local communities are kept abreast of development plans at their local airports.

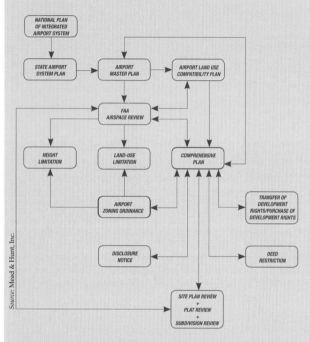

Figure 1.1. *Relationships among Airport-related Planning Techniques*

In a perfect world, planners and airports, usually represented by the airport managers, would have standing lines of communication that provide continual opportunities for interaction and coordination on land-use, planning, and airport-related issues. Unfortunately, the reality in most communities is that this sort of communication does not exist. Planning for local communities and planning for local airports are too often completed through separate efforts, with each making little consideration of the plans or needs of the other. Consequently, the resulting plans are often at odds and can create contradictory approaches to development. To remedy this lack of communication, local planners and airport managers should establish permanent lines of communication that support coordination during specific

planning projects and facilitate day-to-day communication on projects that are important to both groups.

Since the responsibility for land-use planning is delegated to the local level by state and federal agencies, the full burden of addressing land-use issues falls squarely on the shoulders of local planners, elected officials, and appointed committee members. Consequently, it is critical that both the flying public and local residents develop a solid understanding of the importance of compatible land uses near airports, in order to benefit both local communities and the airport as an important transportation and economic development facility.

It is important to be aware that the term "local planners" may apply to more than a single agency. Since an airport's area of influence can extend a considerable distance from its actual property boundaries, multiple municipalities or governmental agencies may be responsible for land-use and planning decisions that affect airport operations or that are influenced by aircraft flying overhead. For example, an airport may be owned by a city government but be located outside of the city limits, within a different municipality or within an area governed by county-level planning controls. In such a case, there are very likely at least two entities that have jurisdiction over land-use and planning decisions, which would need to be taken into consideration. With multiple entities involved, coordination and regulation can easily become very complicated issues.

In addition to establishing permanent communication to support continual dialogue among various agencies, it is also essential to engage these groups in the planning processes. This is a two-way street in that the local airport should invite the relevant municipalities and agencies to partake in the development of airport planning projects, and the local communities should invite airport representatives to be part of their planning efforts. (See Table 1.1 on page 5.) This allows both sides to be heard in different contexts, in relation to the development and needs of both the airport and the greater community.

Airports undertake periodic planning projects, similar to community comprehensive or master planning efforts. The planning process usually results in two documents: a written report, called the master plan report, and the graphic representation of the future development, known as the airport layout plan (ALP). To obtain federal funding, airports must have an ALP on file with the Federal Aviation Administration (FAA). The ALP is discussed further in Chapter 3, and the planning techniques for compatible land uses are surveyed and detailed in Chapter 4.

TABLE 1.1. PLANNING TOOLS FOR COMPATIBLE LAND USES

Tool	Description	Key Value	Primary Shortcoming	When to Use
Comprehensive Plan	Long-term techniques with goals, objectives, maps, charts, and text	Provides for organized community growth and development, including land use and (sometimes) airport elements	Airports and communities do not always plan growth together, thus allowing the encroachment of incompatible land uses into airport environs and vice versa.	Comprehensive plans must be completed by local communities and updated periodically, preferably in conjunction with the airport master plan/airport layout plan (below).
Area Plan	Area-specific techniques with goals and objectives	Addresses specific areas that require more detailed methods to guide land-use regulations, such as areas surrounding airports	It can be difficult to implement and enforce area-specific criteria that control land uses near the airport.	Area plans are typically completed as a follow-on element to the findings or recommendations of a comprehensive plan and may need to be updated to reflect changes or updates to an airport master plan/airport layout plan.
Joint or Regional Planning and Intergovernmental Agreement	Coordinated planning and zoning efforts among multiple jurisdictions to ensure airport viability	Provides roles, responsibilities, and obligations to regulate and plan for airport-compatible land uses	Requires implementing and enforcing land-use controls across multiple jurisdictions, as well as consensus and participation among all jurisdictions affected by airport operations	Such agreements should be utilized to coordinate and plan in multiple jurisdictions that are affected by an airport.
Airport Land-Use Compatibility Plan (ALUCP), including land-use zoning ordinance	Typically a subsection of the comprehensive plan or area plan that addresses airport land-use compatibility goals and objectives	Provides structure and regulations pertaining to community development within the airport's environs; specifically addresses compatibility issues and sets compatibility criteria	Requires implementing and enforcing land-use controls over multiple jurisdictions; the agency preparing an ALUCP may not have sufficient jurisdiction over local land use	Airport land-use compatibility plans should be completed for every jurisdiction affected by an airport.
Airport Master Plan/Airport Layout Plan	Long-term planning document with goals, objectives, maps, charts, and text; typically has a 20-year window for proposed development	Provides guidance for future growth and development of the airport	Addresses only airport growth and development and usually does not consider growth and development in the surrounding communities	Should be utilized to coordinate organized growth and development for both the surrounding communities and the airport; should be evaluated every five years or after significant development has occurred, to assess the progress of development and update accordingly, if necessary
Plan Review	Airport overlay zoning that regulates land uses and height limitations within the airport's environs	Coordinates zoning and regulations that protect the airport from encroachment of incompatible land uses and vice versa	Requires cooperation and implementation from all municipalities involved	Should be utilized to regulate land-use decisions within the airport's environs
Height Zoning Ordinance	Regulation of the height of structures, objects, or natural vegetation within the airport's environs	Eliminates hazardous conditions for aircraft utilizing the airport	Regulates only height concerns and does not address additional safety hazards such as visual obstructions, noise, wildlife and bird attractants, and concentrations of people	Should be utilized in conjunction with or as part of airport overlay zoning ordinance
Site Plan/Plat Review	A set of plans that illustrates the type of development or extent to which a parcel of property will be divided	Contains a detailed description of the parcel of property to be split and the type of proposed development or expansion, location within the parcel of property, material being used, vegetation, et cetera	Municipality does not always address airport needs and concerns prior to approval.	Should be utilized for any new or existing development to ensure that it is airport compatible
Deed Restriction	A legal document attached to the deed or title of a parcel of property that governs use of the property in perpetuity	Restricts use of a parcel of property to ensure land-use compatibility within airport environs	Potential property owners or lessees are not always aware of the restrictions prior to purchase or construction of a hazardous structure, object, or natural vegetation.	Should be utilized within areas affected by airport operations and within aircraft overflight areas; can be required as condition for development approval

• Participating in noise mitigation and other environmental planning processes to ensure an understanding and integration of the findings into community comprehensive plans. (See Chapter 5.)

ENDNOTES

1. Federal Aviation Administration (FAA), advisory circular 150/5070-6B, Airport Master Plans, July 29, 2005 (updated May 1, 2007); available at www.faa.gov/documentLibrary/media/advisory_circular/150-5070-6B/150_5070_6b_chg1.pdf.

2. Stephanie A. D. Ward et al., *Enhancing Airport Land Use Compatibility*, Volume 1: *Land Use Fundamentals and Implementation Resources*. Airport Cooperative Research Program Report 27 (Washington, D.C.: Transportation Research Board, 2010); available at www.trb.org/Main/Blurbs/Enhancing_Airport_Land_Use_Compatibility_Volume_1_163344.aspx.

3. Airport Consultants Council and Federal Aviation Administration, *Improving the Quality of Airport Projects: ACC/FAA Best Practices*, 2008; available at www.acconline.org/Content/NavigationMenu/Resources/ACCLibrary/ACC_FAA_Best_Practice_Final.July08.pdf.

4. Central Region Airports Division, *AIP Sponsor Guide*, September 1, 2009; available at www.faa.gov/airports/central/aip/sponsor_guide/media/0500.pdf.

5. See FAA, advisory circular 150/5070-6B, *Airport Master Plans*, and advisory circular 150/5300, *Airport Design*, available at www.faa.gov/documentLibrary/media/advisory_circular/150-5070-6B/150_5070_6b_chg1.pdf and www.faa.gov/documentLibrary/media/Advisory_Circular/150_5300_13.pdf.

CHAPTER 2

Developing a
Strong Airport Vision

Susan M. Schalk, AICP

 The best mechanism for smooth integration of a community's comprehensive plan and an airport master plan is the visioning process of the airport plan, in which key stakeholders collaborate to establish a vision for the future of the airport that understands and considers its optimal role in the local, regional, and national systems of airports.

This visioning process should be locally driven. A first attempt to articulate a vision for an airport may be a general statement that applies to many airports, such as "become known as first-class airport facility"; however, stronger visions are specific and connect to the common elements in the community's own strategic direction. As an example, an airport that functions primarily as a cargo facility within a metropolitan airport system may identify a more detailed vision, such as "to become an inland port with a plan to link cargo through air, rail, and road facilities." Further, this vision may identify logistical opportunities or synergies with other local industries and economic engines through development of a mission and goals with specific strategies to lead to future development plans. In turn, local users may then be willing to rally around this vision and contribute to its realization.

Although FAA advisory circulars focus on the planning techniques for a systematic process to ensure the effective use of airport resources, successful airport master planning extends beyond planning for facilities. Airports are key components of economic development strategies for communities and regions. The master planning process has evolved from answering questions of "what" and "when" to engaging with other stakeholders to address questions of "how" and "why." It is not enough for an airport to decide to expand because doing so suits its own agenda; that expansion has to resonate with and fulfill the objectives of other significant contributors to the local economy, as well as the communities of which they are a part.

The FAA identifies the first task in an airport master plan process as the creation of a public involvement program, which provides a mechanism through which community planners can have extensive involvement in airport planning processes. According to the FAA, "Public involvement has its greatest impact during the early stages of the planning process, before irreversible decisions have been made."[1] The level of public involvement in airport planning is typically proportional to the complexity of the planning study and the degree of public interest. Typically, provisions for committee involvement are included in the airport master plan process, using technical advisory committees or citizen advisory committees to facilitate public involvement. Members of technical advisory committees provide input and insight on technical issues, and they can include community planners or their representatives, who can provide knowledge about the comprehensive planning for the area surrounding the airport. The airport master planning process may also use a variety of other forums, such as public information meetings, small group meetings, online engagement (through webpages or social media), and other public awareness campaigns to foster community involvement. A strong communication program during the airport master plan requires understanding what the public audience already knows; using everyday language—avoiding acronyms and technical jargon—in order to supply facts; making messages simple, brief, and clear; and avoiding responses that trivialize public concerns.[2]

There are a number of elements in the airport master planning process that demand a strong public outreach program. The airport master plan puts forward resolutions to logistical challenges and introduces potential changes in land use, which many times lead to controversy. Compatible land uses in the immediate area surrounding the runway often require the elimination of residential developments in close proximity to the airfield. For example, one airport's plan led to the development of an active cargo operation, which increased the utilization of the airport

Figure 2.1. Cargo handling is a critical function of many airports.

Columbus Regional Airport Authority

STAKEHOLDER INVOLVEMENT AND AIRPORT PLANNING BUY-IN

Holland Young

Generating stakeholder understanding and buy-in for airport projects is critical to project success. There is a wide array of stakeholder involvement techniques that planners can use and a similarly broad range of interests that must be addressed appropriately.

Developing the Vision, Goals, and Objectives

Developing a well-understood and appropriate vision, set of goals, and objectives for an airport project is critical to the project's success. Doing this not only will allow the airport sponsor to develop and sustain stakeholder support over the life of the project but also will provide the basis for good project planning.

Typically, the vision will form the central theme for all communications regarding the "future of the airport." The vision, together with the goals and objectives, provides the framework for positioning the project at hand—typically one focused on the airport's present and envisioned capacity needs—as a necessary component for achieving this future. The vision statement should be developed based on agreed-upon goals and objectives that work to support and amplify the important aspects of the project.

Vision. A concise and focused statement, typically defining the role of the airport in the local, regional, and global transportation networks, while reflecting local and regional values.

Goals. Specific statements expanding upon the defined vision to guide future airport development. Capacity needs should be addressed here.

Objectives. Under each goal, objectives identify the specific items that are important to achieve; the best objectives are measurable using established criteria. Specific capacity solutions are addressed here.

To develop the vision, goals, and objectives, project proponents must:

- Understand the role of the airport in the social and economic life of the community
- Understand the current and historical airport-community relationship
- Understand stakeholder interests
- Build a common knowledge platform
- Understand the forces at play
- Carefully assess geographic considerations
- Stay focused to achieve consensus
- Address all community sectors
- Build support through project committees

The Role of the Airport in the Social and Economic Life of the Community

Airports come in a wide array of sizes and locations and serve an even wider variety of communities, from large metropolitan areas to smaller regional cities. Each community's specific need for air service depends on the size of its population and the needs and nature of its economic base. If an airport's vision is to resonate with local and, especially, regional audiences and stakeholders, it must reflect the realities of the airport's role in the social and economic life of the communities it serves. Specific large-scale infrastructure projects, while easily justified on a technical basis, can be met with resistance due to the reluctance of the local community to accept further expansions of flights, noise, congestion, or pollution. The need to build new airport capacity is usually tied to a region's population growth and expansion or articulation of its economic base. Helping stakeholders understand this connection and the importance of the airport and other transportation infrastructure to the region's economic health is critical. Conversely, the economic value of a community's quality of life—which expansion can affect—needs to be considered as well.

Overcoming or accommodating local reservations cannot be achieved through technical discussions alone. Building support for large-scale infrastructure projects can best be achieved through a clear statement of a vision indicating where the airport is going and how that relates to the social and economic future of the community or region.

The Current and Historical Airport-Community Relationship

Airport projects are a key to the future success of the airport and its ability to meet community needs. A vision should be supported by goals and objectives that are formulated through a carefully executed dialogue with the affected communities.

In planning for an airport project, an airport sponsor develops its technical requirements. These are typically objective and analytical, as they support plans that must be viable in terms of finances, operations, environmental considerations, and construction. The technical aspects of capacity projects should be well understood by airport management, who should also be well versed in the alternatives to the project and the issues associated with its implementation. A purpose and need statement should encapsulate this technical aspect of a capacity project. Developing this project information well is critically important to support the defined vision.

An understanding of the current conditions and future potential of a given region is necessary in order to comprehend the driving factors behind community values. Each community has a unique range of values and attributes that must be understood and incorporated into discussions with community stakeholders about the vision and benefits of the capacity project. While many of these community aspects will be somewhat subjective and more difficult to measure (e.g., quality of life), understanding the potential future of the region is critical to developing the most appropriate vision for the airport.

(continued on page 10)

(continued from page 9)

Stakeholder Interests

Stakeholders typically span a wide array of interests and involvement, and effectively addressing these diverse interests can be challenging. In addition, differing levels of knowledge about the airport and the need for a capacity project further complicate the effective dialogue. (This is discussed further below.) Successfully generating support relies on understanding stakeholder interests and concerns and effectively using common issues and targeted messages in a comprehensive communications strategy.

Airport operators must satisfy the regulatory requirements across local, state, and federal entities that have approval and advisory authority. The issues of other public entities that may not have approval authority, such as transit agencies, should also be addressed, because these agencies can generate project support.

Community groups and other nongovernmental organizations are perhaps the most challenging because their concerns may vary widely, ranging from business and financial interest to concern for personal and family well-being.

A Common Knowledge Platform

In addition to taking into account the wide range of issues and specific agendas, it is important to understand the level of knowledge among stakeholders, as this varies widely as well. Effectively dealing with preconceived notions and "urban legends" about the airport and capacity needs is critical. For example, in some locations stakeholders believe that relocating all general aviation and cargo activity from a busy hub airport will provide sufficient future capacity, even though these activities may not consume a significant portion of the airport capacity and there is no legal authority to make these users move. A common base of knowledge among the stakeholders can serve as a platform for rational and coherent discourse. Generally, an effective education program will result in a common understanding of the issues at play and the interdependent needs of the airport and the community.

The Forces at Play

A wide range of forces within the community can influence the overall level of support for any given capacity project. To effectively generate support, project proponents must understand and appropriately harness these forces.

Some of the rationales that typically underlie an airport expansion or other capacity solution include increased activity at the airport, the nearing of current capacity limitations, and the need to sustain the regional economy. These considerations should be quantified and their importance demonstrated to stakeholders throughout the dialogue.

Conversely, there are numerous factors that can work against implementation of a capacity project. These usually involve regulatory issues, political concerns, and technical factors. Addressing all regulatory requirements can involve negotiating with multiple controlling entities (such as local and regional governmental entities and councils of government) and can limit both the range of solutions and the suitability of specific implementation methods. Political factors can introduce unrelated issues, including preconceived yet inaccurate notions, and can place stakeholders in a defensive mode, which works against consensus building. This is especially noticeable during an election cycle, when candidates who have little understanding of aviation issues seize upon a "banner" issue (e.g., airport noise) and proclaim that it can be solved by voting for the candidate. The truth is that airport noise is a significant issue, but dealing effectively with it requires knowledge of the airport operating environment, regulatory aspects, and the community's development history.

The technical factors involved with any capacity-enhancing project can be complicated, leading to a difficult dialogue, primarily because it can be challenging to address these issues in a soundbite format. However, in articulating the needs of a project, proponents should take into consideration existing conditions, regional demand characteristics, and cost-benefit analyses. Similarly, community-based planners need to commit to educating themselves about some of the technical complexities that underlie the airport's objectives and proposed method of proceeding.

Geographic Considerations

Airport capacity projects provide benefits across extensive geographic regions. However, the adverse impacts of a project often occur more locally, creating tensions with communities that must be addressed. These tensions can vary depending on distance from the airport or on the nature of a given community, which itself can be shaped by the community's geography.

- *Close-in communities.* The areas closest to an airport capacity project typically bear the highest level of potential impacts. Dialogue with people representing these areas should emphasize any proposed mitigation as well as any long-term impacts on property values. Moreover, local representatives may be able to contribute knowledge or potential impact remedies that airport planners should take into consideration in planning a capacity project.

- *Midvicinity areas.* Beyond the immediate airport area, there is usually a band of communities that experience some impacts (usually significantly reduced in comparision to close-in communities), but mitigation often will not be available this far from the airport. It is important to understand the nature of communities in this situation and work with them to maximize the regional benefits of the project.

- *Regions.* The regional community will often be in the best position to support an airport capacity project, but mobilizing action across a wide area that includes distant communities is difficult. For these areas, it is highly important for airport planners to stress the vision of the project and why it supports the regional future, something that regional planners can help them model and visualize.

facility, resulted in improved airport revenues, and demanded changes in the adjacent land uses to minimize the number of residents living with increased noise levels. The vision for an airport may encompass competing interests; for example, a proposed improvement that places safety first may not complement a desire for reducing the airport's environmental footprint, yet the vision for the airport may incorporate both a safety-first goal and a conflicting sustainability goal. These sorts of competing interests require strong communication that provides a high level of education and encourages discussion that seeks solutions. For instance, meeting airport design requirements for clear areas off the runway ends (areas free of obstacles, known as the runway safety areas) may require the shifting of a runway, thereby increasing the runway footprint.

In summary, the master plan process is typically built on the foundation of a vision for the airport's future. Early participation by community planners in the airport master plan visioning process provides easy access and opportunities to link the community vision with the airport vision. Further, the public outreach process for airport planning benefits from community planner involvement, especially when the creation of a clear message about the airport planning initiatives incorporates familiar language to encourage daily community conversations.

ACHIEVING CONSENSUS

Many airport capacity projects will require political and regulatory approval. These can come in the form of votes by a governing body, such as a city council or county commission, or public referendums. Political entities are sensitive to the needs and concerns of the community, and it is important for project proponents to maintain the appropriate focus on the needs of each.

Columbus Regional Airport Authority

- *Political requirements.* Political stakeholders have a responsibility to the community to minimize impacts while improving the region. Therefore, it is important to correctly identify community concerns and directly address them to obtain support. It should be noted that community and political acceptance are often symbiotic, as each influences the other.

- *Community acceptance.* Addressing community concerns with political individuals allows them to assist in leading the community to support a capacity project that they agree is in the community interest. Community acceptance requires an appropriate explanation of both the benefits and the impacts of these projects.

- *Consensus to move forward.* Aligning political and community interests sets the stage for consensus. This strategy generates the broad-based support for implementation that can be sustained over the life of the project.

COMMUNITY SECTORS THAT BENEFIT FROM AIRPORT EXPANSION

Across the region there are a wide range of sectors that have an interest in or see a potential benefit from a given airport capacity project. Involving these

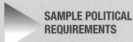

SAMPLE POLITICAL
REQUIREMENTS

Austin-Bergstrom International Airport

New Airport—1993

- Affordable
- Environmentally favorable
- Suitable for use given neighborhood concerns

San Diego International Airport

Destination Lindbergh—2008

- Determine the ultimate build-out configuration of San Diego International Airport
- Evaluate and plan to minimize airport-related traffic impacts to adjacent communities
- Improve intermodal access to the airport, while considering the airport as a potential location for a regional transportation hub

Portland International Airport

Airport Futures—2010

- Allow the city to address the complex issues associated with the airport and its potential impacts
- Provide the community with a greater opportunity to influence airport planning and development
- Provide the port with flexibility to respond to changing circumstances in airport development

sectors is recommended, as together they can achieve synergies and have a cumulative impact on the process. The mutual recognition of the importance of the airport acts to reinforce the participation of each sector and its representatives' willingness to go on record before the appropriate political bodies that decide on aspects of the airport projects. Achieving the right level of involvement from each sector is a key goal to obtain both support and input.

- *Local and regional planning organizations.* This sector typically involves planning agencies and institutional research groups that are focused on large-scale planning issues (transportation, economic development, community development and housing, regional land use, and environmental policy) associated with population growth. Project proponents will benefit from establishing relationships with planners and leaders in these organizations and partnering with them to develop support. These entities often have a good understanding of community stakeholders and their concerns and can help airport sponsors effectively engage their constituents.

- *Environment.* This sector covers a wide range of stakeholders and audiences, from government agencies to garden clubs and from recreational groups to conservation organizations. The local, state, and federal regulatory bodies charged with the protection of the environment, as well as environmental advocacy groups, should be engaged early in the project development process in order to address concerns and facilitate communication.

- *Military.* This sector covers all branches of the military. Its influence varies widely in different metropolitan areas and cities, as some have a relatively small military presence, while others have a very large and important military community.

- *Economic development and business.* These stakeholders and airport users are likely beneficiaries of the capacity enhancement and are key proponents to assist project sponsors in building support.

- *Transportation and logistics.* Airports are one of the five modes in a regional transportation network. (The others are roads, rails, transit, and water.) This sector covers a very wide range of both public and private large- and small-scale transportation entities. Multimodal connections between airports and other transportation modes are increasingly important to regional economic growth in terms of both passenger transport and freight and goods movement. New capacity projects may address such connections either on their own or as part of a larger undertaking.

- *Education.* This sector includes three basic components: the primary and secondary school systems, community and technical colleges, and four-year colleges and universities. Recognizing potential academic resources and their stakeholder roles is important, as they have the potential to be strong advocates or opponents, as well as sources of information.

- *Health and human services.* This sector includes the major hospitals and medical research centers that often depend on air service for both patients and other business relationships. Therefore, capacity projects can be an asset to the business activities of this sector.

- *Tourism, conventions, and professional sports events.* This sector covers a wide variety of public agencies and private businesses that all are highly dependent on the airport for their success.

- *Culture, arts, and history.* This sector is involved with visual and performing arts, which often have facilities and operations that depend on air service for visiting artists and performers, as well as audiences that are willing to travel to see and participate in various cultural and arts activities. Because these entities have a large stake in enhancing a region's airport capacity, engaging them early to promote project benefits is important. They can also provide valuable information about anticipated cultural growth in the region, which can affect economic health and travel demand.

- *Real estate and development.* This community includes commercial and residential real-estate developers, brokers, and financers. People in this arena are highly aware of the importance of the airport to the growth of the community. Capacity projects may benefit the real-estate industry in the immediate vicinity of the airport by enhancing the market for aviation-related and other businesses. The importance of these potential benefits should not be underestimated in gaining community support. People in this sector can also provide in-depth analysis of expected growth trends and demand drivers.

- *Governance and public management.* This sector involves city councils, county commissions, elected representatives, and the primary managers of the city and the county. Elected officials and other key public officials can spread project messages broadly across the local and regional community, as well as elicit important information from those communities. It is critically important to brief those stakeholders early and often to keep the core project messages on track and to head off potentially fatal project opposition from this sector.

PROJECT COMMITTEES

In formulating the project and determining the best alternative, there is a significant opportunity to gain trust and build support through committee involvement. Similar types of stakeholders can be grouped by nature and level of engagement to allow the most effective discussions. However, cross-pollination across stakeholder sectors also can be highly effective in bringing out valuable differing points of view for consideration.

Committees facilitate the implementation of a civic engagement strategy that aggregates sectors and geographic representation, fosters education, and allows a dialogue on community issues and the important aspects of the airport capacity project. Types of committees that can be helpful include:

- *Policy.* Advises on the future of the region and the vision that the airport should have to support that future (very high level perspective)

- *Technical.* Advises on technical matters relating to specific airport plans and concepts (down into the weeds on technical matters)

- *Community.* Advises on community concerns, goals, and plans as inputs to the airport plans (moderate-level perspective)

COMMON THEMES

Common themes that arise across stakeholder interests should be observed and harnessed. These themes often form an effective framework for the dialogue that leads to the best vision, goals, and objectives.

One of the most effective ways to generate ideas and identify these themes is to conduct a series of individual and small-group meetings with stakeholders, where the discussion can be more informal and varied. During these discussions, the project proponents should seek to understand not only needs and concerns but how these issues can best be addressed.

CONCLUSIONS ABOUT THE ROLE OF STAKEHOLDERS IN THE VISIONING PROCESS

- There is no substitute for targeted community involvement at the appropriate stages, and early involvement is critical to generating support and garnering information for capacity projects.

- Vision, goals, and objectives form the foundation for good planning and communications about capacity projects.

- The best vision, goals, and objectives come from a clear understanding of the community, which is a complex and multifaceted undertaking.

- Developing the right vision, goals, and objectives sets up the plan for implementation.

CASE STUDY: CRYSTAL CITY PLAN FEASIBILITY STUDY, ARLINGTON, VIRGINIA
Planning for Redevelopment near Ronald Reagan Washington National Airport
Alex Iams

Arlington County planners collaborated with local landowners and airspace authorities to solve a complex problem: how to reconcile plans for dozens of new buildings (some exceeding 300 feet) with safe and fluid operations at a major airport that is within walking distance of the new development. Complicating matters, it was also necessary to consider the effects on radar coverage in the sensitive airspace nearby and westward into the Virginia countryside.

Figure 2.2. Crystal City, with Ronald Reagan Washington National Airport behind it.

Arlington Economic Development

Arlington's 50-year plan for the redevelopment of Crystal City is ambitious. It calls for the replacement of approximately 30 existing buildings with more than 55 new ones, adding some 15.5 million square feet of net density to the 24 million square feet already in existence. Failure to address the legitimate issues with this plan that were raised by the Metropolitan Washington Airports Authority (MWAA) and the Federal Aviation Administration (FAA) could have stalled or derailed the redevelopment.

In the airspace evaluation process, Arlington planners learned about such arcane terms as Part 77s, TERPS, and Fused Tracking Radar, while the FAA got familiar with long-term community planning concepts. In time, each team provided the knowledge—land-use plan data from the county, modeling technology from the FAA—needed to complete the project. The outcome of the analysis is mutually-beneficial: a long-term land-use plan that is closely coordinated with airspace interests.

About Crystal City and the FAA Feasibility Study
Situated between the Pentagon and Ronald Reagan Washington National Airport (DCA), Crystal City commands one of the best locations in the capital region. With a crewcut skyline, Crystal City looks like the kind of downtown

one might expect to see near an airport. But with new buildings and a more urban future on the way, the relationships between Crystal City and the airport had to be revisited.

The Crystal City Plan is a countermeasure to the federal Base Realignment and Closure (BRAC) action of 2005. BRAC moves defense-related federal agencies out of urban locales—which tend to be ill-suited for post–September 11 security standards such as 82-foot setbacks—and into less dense environments and military installations. Because of BRAC, Crystal City is scheduled to lose 13,000 employees and the occupancy of 3.2 million square feet of office space.

The county was determined to plan for the next generation of development in Crystal City, but it needed to ensure that future development would not run afoul of FAA standards or imperil the safety and integrity of operations at the airport. Wherever standards could not be met, mitigations would have to be planned for the anticipated conflicts.

At the beginning of the land-use planning process, the county and the largest property owner (Vornado Charles E. Smith) enlisted MWAA and the FAA to evaluate the plan. Together these groups produced a feasibility study, also known as a broad area assessment, of existing and future development in Crystal City.

The feasibility study positions the county to adopt its long-term land-use plan with a firm understanding of

(1) how each future building would be viewed by the FAA under its normal single-building evaluation;

(2) the cumulative impact of the buildings on air traffic, navigation, communications, and surveillance systems, as projected over 15 years; and

(3) recommended mitigations to accompany certain buildings and the area at large.

The FAA Building Review Process

At airports across the United States, the FAA establishes virtual obstacle surfaces designed to protect the airport—and more broadly the National Airspace System—from encroachments that would limit operations. These surfaces are established through Federal Aviation Regulation Part 77, Objects Affecting Navigable Airspace.

As stated in FAA procedures for handling airspace matters, "a structure that exceeds one or more of Part 77 standards is a presumed hazard to air navigation unless the obstruction evaluation study determines otherwise." The Part 77 surface can generally be described as a conical or tiered surface in the air, rising with the distance from the airport. In addition, development must be balanced against the surfaces established by the U.S. Standard for Terminal Instrument Procedures (TERPS), which pilots use to navigate between airports and make safe arrivals and departures.

When a development project is planned near an airport, the real estate developer (or developer representative, typically an aviation consultant) must submit an FAA Form 7460, which the FAA uses to review the project information. If a proposed structure exceeds a Part 77 standard, it automatically triggers a detailed aeronautical study intended to further evaluate the structure based on TERPS and other potential areas of conflict.

The study passes through FAA divisions specializing in air traffic; airports; flight procedures and flight standards; airway facilities; and military branch interests. Each team examines the potential impacts to their area of responsibility before the FAA makes a determination. A determination identifies any impacts the building would cause and what changes to the use of the airspace or to the proposed building would be required to mitigate the obstruction.

Sometimes, the changes are relatively minor and with the proper technical adjustments can be implemented without concerning the aeronautical community. However, if an obstruction would cause substantial impacts (known as "adverse effects") to safety, operations, efficiency, national security, or another critical function, which would affect a certain volume of air traffic, the FAA will declare the obstruction a hazard.

Feasibility Study Process and Findings

The feasibility study process took place through a series of working sessions held in Washington, D.C., with participants from the FAA, the U.S. Air Force, DCA air-traffic control, MWAA, and the National Security Agency. Arlington County staff from the planning and economic development units attended the working sessions to answer questions about the proposed buildings and timing.

The working group decided to focus on conditions during the first 15 years (2011–2025) of redevelopment. The 15-year period was subdivided into three five-year increments, allowing technicians to identify specific buildings affecting the airspace. Using the building data provided by Arlington County, the FAA and the Air Force modeled the impacts. The Air Force brought in the technology needed to assess radar coverage. All impacts were reviewed, including navigation, radar, flight procedures, radio communications, and review by the armed forces. Special consideration was given to the cumulative impacts of the buildings on radar coverage.

Initial results showed that some of the tallest proposed buildings would likely produce radar shadows in pockets of airspace northwest of the Washington area such that mitigation would become necessary. The working group devised several mitigation scenarios (for example, a new location for the existing radar and overlay of a new surveillance technology) under which the proposed development could be re-evaluated. After testing those scenarios, the results were issued in the feasibility study report.

The report includes the effects of the buildings (individually and collectively) on regional airspace and operations. The impacts on TERPS from each building are noted in the report, along with direction for potential mitigations; they are to be addressed during the future aeronautical-review process when a developer files a project with the FAA. The impacts to TERPS do not suggest a need to adjust planned building heights, provided the proposed mitigations are pursued when the project is filed.

In terms of radar coverage, the buildings analyzed for the first increment will not impair radar services currently provided to air-traffic operations in the region. Buildings in the second and third increments will require a technology called radar-track fusion between the radar at DCA and a regional installation called Potomac Tracon. This technology joins the capacity of multiple radar signals into one view, filling any gaps affecting a single installation. An operational radar-track fusion function at DCA would resolve the shadowing issues caused by buildings in the second and third five-year increments.

Radar-track fusion is planned for implementation at DCA in three to five years. Track fusion is an initial step in the transition to Global Positioning Systems (GPS) technology, which will ultimately replace radar at airports around the country as the primary airspace surveillance tool. Representatives from the FAA and the county will meet periodically to update the progress of development and the status of new technologies.

What Makes the Crystal City Study Distinctive?

It evaluates a plan, not a building. Each of the proposed Crystal City buildings was evaluated according to the standard FAA aeronautical-review process outlined above. However, this study looked at an entire collection of planned buildings and their impacts over time, based on a projected build-out schedule.

It comprehensively assesses radar coverage. The study is groundbreaking for the assessment of cumulative impacts on the radar coverage from DCA. While a typical aeronautical study evaluates radar impacts for the building under review, it would not necessarily join those impact to those from nearby or proposed buildings—and it definitely would not project impacts 15 years into the future. It is the cumulative impacts that should most concern planners, because under the current system it is not possible to foresee problems until the next marginal development project causes the entire area to cross a threshold of concern. By assessing cumulative impacts on radar coverage, the Crystal City study unlocked critical pieces of information needed to determine both the plan's viability as well as the potential technology needed to address impacts.

It links to future building reviews. Setting expectations today will allow future building evaluations near the time of construction to be processed more smoothly. The Form 7460 applications accompanying new construction will track back to the feasibility study. This linkage assures the county, the FAA, and real estate developers that this series of buildings can be pursued within the recommended mitigations outlined in the study.

It provides context for the aeronautical review. Representatives from the FAA shared the county's sense that this project charted new territory in the way the agency works with local communities. For those on the FAA side, it may have been the first time they heard about how buildings fit into a larger plan and why the plan is important to the community—in Arlington's case, on account of the economic concerns raised by BRAC. On the county side, planners gained an appreciation for the complexity inherent in managing and protecting the airspace. Face-to-face meetings facilitated the communication of these concepts.

Integral Prerequisites

Have a concept plan and an economic analysis. Before any planned buildings could be evaluated in the feasibility study, Arlington had to develop an illustrative concept plan for Crystal City. This planning process took several years, requiring dozens of community meetings, technical inputs, and hefty staff commitments from divisions across the county government, as well as consultant assistance for master planning, economic analysis, and transportation analysis.

During the planning process, Arlington Economic Development (AED) prepared economic analyses to test whether the amounts and types of development planned could be built and absorbed and estimated when the construction would be likely to occur. The economic analysis turned out to be a critical component of the FAA review. One of the first hurdles overcome in working with the FAA was to convey that redevelopment in Crystal City would occur incrementally, rather than all at once. The market analysis showed which buildings would be built and when.

The concept plan, plotted to the building footprint level, allowed the county to show exactly where buildings would be located and how tall they would be, from ground level and from sea level. The timing of construction, based on the AED analysis, was shown in three five-year increments. This allowed airspace conditions to be measured at the five-, 10-, and 15-year marks. It also allowed the FAA to test the buildings against the technologies that would be available at different points in the future. This was tremendously important for identifying when a new technology would be needed. For example, the study found that the Phase One buildings could be built without substantial changes to the surveillance technology, whereas Phase Two buildings would require some changes.

Build and maintain a relationship with the FAA. The project would not have gotten started without building a relationship with the FAA, a process that began before the Crystal City project. Arlington's location near the agency headquarters in Washington, D.C., had enabled previous face-to-face meetings related to individual building proposals between county staff and FAA personnel. When the Crystal City study came along, Arlington already had relationships with the agency and a mutual understanding that looking at all of the buildings at once would save everybody's time in the future.

In addition, Arlington took advantage of its existing partnerships with MWAA and the local real estate development community. Like Arlington, these groups had prior relationships with the FAA and knowledge of the agency structure. MWAA provided the FAA with any information needed about the airport, such as physical layout, future plans, and the obstacles and opportunities related to improving operations and surveillance. MWAA representatives attended every meeting and joined every conference call. MWAA and the county have worked well together, recognizing the overlaps between a prosperous community and a prosperous airport.

The primary landowner, Vornado Charles E. Smith, and its aviation consultant, Ben Doyle of JDA Aviation Technology Solutions, helped tremendously with the educational aspects of the aeronautical review process, potential mitigations, new surveillance technologies, and FAA agency structure. The landowner will eventually build many of the proposed buildings, so it was critical to have its buy-in on the evaluation and how it would match up with its plans.

All three local groups—Arlington County, MWAA, and the landowner—were key to securing the FAA's participation in the study. Once the study began, it was critical to stay on the often difficult path toward a solution rather than the easier path to rejection. This was accomplished by stressing the benefits for each side. For the county, it was a chance to advance a long-term land-use plan compatible with airport and airspace interests; and for the FAA, it was an opportunity to settle many individual issues at once and to create a model for addressing community plans elsewhere.

Keys to Success

While the right approach to working with the FAA cannot be boiled down to a formula, this particular project was successful because Arlington County took the following actions:

- Developed a conceptual plan for the long-term future of Crystal City with enough detail to know where buildings will be located and how tall they will be;

- Completed an economic analysis to determine when buildings are likely to be built;

- Built and maintained relationships with local partners, such as the airports authority and the real estate developer, and joined efforts with them to engage the FAA;

- Nurtured a mutual understanding of county goals and FAA goals by sharing information and educating counterparts; and

- Established a framework for follow-up interactions between the county and the FAA regarding the project.

Completing the feasibility study process with the FAA allows Arlington to move forward with its plans for Crystal City. The study moves the county closer to reinventing an important downtown and provides the assurance that future building reviews will trace back to this evaluation.

CASE STUDY: DESTINATION LINDBERGH: COLLABORATION AND VISION TO MEET THE REGION'S MOBILITY NEEDS

Robert A. Leiter, FAICP, Keith Wilschetz, and Tait Galloway

Destination Lindbergh was a year-long, comprehensive planning process designed to: (1) determine the ultimate build-out configuration of San Diego International Airport (SDIA) at Lindbergh Field; (2) minimize airport-related traffic impacts on adjacent communities; and (3) improve intermodal access to the airport, while considering the airport as a location for a regional transportation hub. In order to address the three priorities comprehensively, Destination Lindbergh was an integrated, regional surface- and air-transportation planning effort.

A breakthrough alliance of the San Diego County Regional Airport Authority, the City of San Diego, and the San Diego Association of Governments (SANDAG) formed the Ad Hoc Airport Regional Policy Committee, chaired by San Diego mayor Jerry Sanders. The committee also invited policy makers from the San Diego Unified Port District, the County of San Diego, the Metropolitan Transit System, the North County Transit District, and the U.S. Department of Defense.

Goals and Objectives

A wide range of goals and objectives reflecting regional priorities were developed through discussions with the committee. The goals of Destination Lindbergh are:

- Improve direct access by autos and various modes of transit to SDIA and accommodate vehicle parking demand

- Develop an intermodal facility to provide access for passengers and employees to SDIA and strengthen regional connectivity

- Develop passenger terminal facilities to efficiently accommodate projected passenger demand and enhance user satisfaction

- Within the constraints of SDIA's property and single runway, develop an airfield configuration to best accommodate projected levels of aircraft operations

- Incorporate best practices of environmental stewardship in all components of SDIA's physical environment and operations

- Develop a financially feasible plan

- Leverage SDIA to provide major direct and indirect social and economic benefits

- Integrate SDIA, through context-sensitive urban design, into the fabric of the central San Diego area

Existing Airport Facilities

SDIA is approximately three miles northwest of downtown San Diego and comprises 661 acres. It features a single 9,400-foot long east-west runway that is supported by a full-length parallel taxiway on the south and a partial-length parallel taxiway on the north (Figure 2.3, page 20). The airport has three passenger terminals, providing a total of 41 gates. Support facilities, including the fuel farm, air traffic control tower, and cargo and general aviation facilities, are located primarily north of the runway.

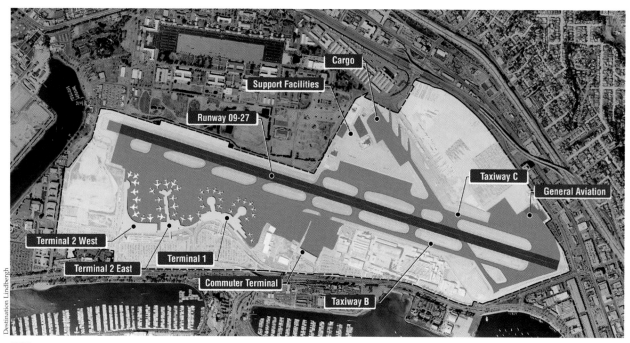

Destination Lindbergh

LEGEND

⌐ ¬ Airport property boundary	▢ Existing terminal
▮ Runway	▮ Airline/ Airport support

Figure 2.3. Existing facilities at San Diego International Airport

Existing Transit Facilities

Transit service to the airport from downtown San Diego is provided by a Metropolitan Transit System bus ("The Flyer"). The downtown terminus provides connections to the region's light-rail and bus system. There is currently no direct rail access to the airport, so preparation of this plan presented a great opportunity to develop this long-needed connection.

Overview of Destination Lindbergh Plan

The purpose of Destination Lindbergh was to strategize the ultimate build-out of Lindbergh Field, review the potential for an intermodal transportation center (ITC), and determine actions that could reduce traffic on surrounding arterial streets. In addition, the study assessed the feasibility of direct access ramps from Interstate 5 (I-5) to the ITC.

Scenario Development

Since Lindbergh Field is generally oriented east-west and is bisected by a single runway, there are opportunities for increased ground access from rail lines and I-5 in the northeast corner of the airport. Three broad site-planning scenarios emerged during the study process:

- A scenario with a single entrance to the airport on the north side of the airfield, with all airline processing functions (ticketing, check-in, and baggage) and gates, as well as an ITC and direct I-5 access along the rail corridor south of Washington Street.

- A scenario in which the gates remain on the south side of the runway but access is provided in the north and a connection made to the south via an internal road or a people-mover system.

- A hybrid scenario in which ground access and airline processing was developed on both the north and south sides of the airport. Connection of the ITC and gates on the north to gates on the south would be made via a people mover.

Recommended Development Plan and Phasing

The recommended development plan most closely resembled the south-centric scenario. (See Figure 2.4.) In the final build-out all access to the airport processing functions would be provided north of the runway with a people-mover connection to redeveloped terminals on the south. Elements of the plan include: development of an ITC allowing connections with rail (intercity, commuter, and high-speed), trolley, and bus (local service and future regional Bus Rapid Transit service), direct I-5 ramp access, a consolidated rental-car facility (CONRAC), and parking garages. Passenger processing would be adjacent to the ITC. A total of 62 gates would be reconstructed on the south side of the runway.

Implementing this plan would likely require 20 to 25 years. Construction timing would depend on additional financial feasibility analysis, environmental, engineering, and design work. Destination Lindbergh recommends three phases:

- *1 (2015–2020).* This phase would include development of rail platforms, additional track work, bus bays, and a grade-separated pedestrian crossing onto airport property from an ITC. The CONRAC facility and additional parking would be built concurrently. Connection from parking, CONRAC, and the ITC to the south side terminals would be made via a shuttle bus on airport property. I-5 access would be improved through

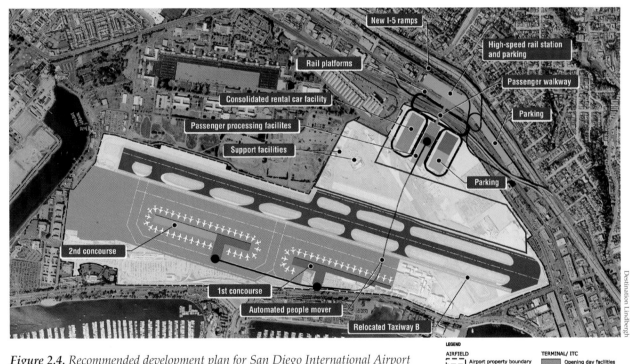

Figure 2.4. *Recommended development plan for San Diego International Airport*

LEGEND

AIRFIELD
- ⌐ ⌐ ⌐ Airport property boundary
- ▨ Existing pavement
- ▨ Future pavement
- ▨ Apron

TERMINAL/ ITC
- ▨ Opening day facilities
- ▨ PAL1 facilities
- ▨ PAL2 facilities
- —— Potential APM alignment
- ● APM station

greater use of existing ramps to the south of the facility and improvements to Sassafras Street and the Pacific Coast Highway in the area of the ITC and CONRAC.

- *2 - 2020 Planning Activity Level 1 timeframe.* Direct access ramps from I-5 would be added as well as a people mover replacing the shuttle-bus connection. Passenger processing would be added to the north-side facility. Direct access to the south-side terminals would remain.

- *3 - 2030 Planning Activity Level 2 timeframe.* Access and processing would be completed to the north side. North Harbor Drive would no longer provide access to passenger-processing facilities, and direct access ramps from I-5 would be completed. During this phase, North Harbor Drive would be used to access only airport support and potential long-term parking facilities.

Increased Transit Use at an ITC

Approximately 1.3 percent of airport passengers currently use transit to SDIA. Current efforts by the Airport Authority and other regional transportation agencies are designed to increase that to 4 to 5 percent over the next 10 years. Analysis by SANDAG as part of Destination Lindbergh indicated potential to increase the use of transit at the airport even further through development of an ITC, to somewhere in the range of 8.5 to 13.0 percent by 2030. If shared-ride van and high-speed rail numbers are included, the range increases to between 15.5 and 21.0 percent (from the current 9.3 percent). This level is comparable to those at the Oakland and San Francisco airports.

Further analysis indicated that an ITC would also result in an increase in nonairport transit trips within the region and could function as an independent facility. However, locating an ITC at this location provides a unique opportunity to capture airport-bound passengers.

Financial Considerations

Initial analysis concludes that a Phase 1 ITC/CONRAC/Parking facility could be financially feasible and function effectively as an independent improvement. Further analysis is needed to determine the viability of the Phase 2 and 3 improvements. Total capital costs are estimated at $3.8 billion (in 2009 dollars), with $457 million of that required for the first phase.

For implementation of Phase 1, a variety of potential funding sources have been identified, including Transportation Infrastructure Finance Innovation Act (TIFIA) loans, Airport Improvement Program grants, Passenger Facility Charges, tax increment financing, and a variety of federal, state, and local funding sources.

Next Steps

In spring 2009, the Destination Lindbergh Plan was accepted by the City of San Diego, the Airport Authority, and SANDAG. With the Airport Authority moving ahead with its Terminal 2 expansion project along with advanced planning for the CONRAC facility, SANDAG has undertaken advanced planning for the ITC Phase 1 improvements. This work will entail developing and evaluating alternatives for the ITC station layout, developing capital-cost estimates (including right-of-way needs), outlining a ground access plan, refining transit-ridership estimates, evaluating opening-day traffic level-of-service impacts, developing a preliminary environmental assessment, and outlining a financial funding plan and implementation schedule. This advanced planning study will be completed by December 2010 and will set the stage for formal environmental studies.

Destination Lindbergh also includes long-term plans for direct ramps connecting I-5 to the proposed north-side airport terminal. Developing detailed capital costs for the ramps will enable SANDAG to seek federal funding in the future multiyear transportation reauthorization bill and annual appropriations processes. This study effort will require conceptual-level engineering and is scheduled for completion by June 2011.

In addition to long-term access and roadway improvements, future land uses and urban form for the area surrounding the ITC will need to be considered. Destination Lindbergh calls for the ITC to be located off airport property, in the Midway Pacific Highway Corridor Community Plan area just south of Washington Street. In fall 2010, the City of San Diego began the update of the Midway Pacific Highway Corridor Community Plan. As part of the community plan update process, the city will work with SANDAG, the Airport Authority, the community, and other stakeholders to consider land use and mobility-integration aspects related to the ITC and the long-term vision of the area's urban form.

CONCLUSIONS

Destination Lindbergh has set forth a vision for a multimodal transportation project that will provide opportunities for increased transit ridership, reduced street traffic and greenhouse gas emissions, and optimized operational capacity within the airfield and property constraints. While not the initial focus of the study, it also became clear as the study proceeded that the ITC could provide an excellent future location for the downtown San Diego terminus of the California High Speed Rail System, which will ultimately connect San Diego to Los Angeles, the Central Valley, and the San Francisco Bay Area. At the same time, the planning process has laid the groundwork for continued collaboration among the many stakeholders.

ENDNOTES

1. Federal Aviation Administration (FAA), advisory circular 150/5070-6B, airport master plans, July 29, 2005 (updated May 1, 2007); available at www.faa.gov/documentLibrary/media/advisory_circular/150-5070-6B/150_5070_6b_chg1.pdf.

2. KB Environmental Sciences, "Closing the Communication Gap: The Right People, Using the Right Words, at the Right Time," *Airport Consulting*, spring 2010; available at www.ACConline.org/Content/NavigationMenu/CurrentACCNews/AirportConsulting/default.htm.

CHAPTER 3

Envisioning Potential Futures through Airport Master Planning

Susan M. Schalk, AICP

 Airport planners and community planners need to partner early in planning processes in order to weave the airport's vision, strategies, and values together with the community's. In this chapter, four additional opportunities that extend beyond the visioning process are identified for community planner participation during the course of the preparation or update of the airport master plan. These opportunities occur in the following planning tasks, with areas of interest for community planners outlined below.

- *Forecasting future aviation demand.* Airport planning techniques are often driven by the need for FAA approval and funding. The FAA perspective may differ from local community projections of growth potential. The reasons why this is so are described in this chapter. Community planners come to the table as a strong socioeconomic resource for the modeling of local projections.

- *Identifying facility requirements to meet aviation demands.* Best practices in sizing and laying out aviation facilities may conflict with competing interests. For instance, safety or capacity guidelines for expanded facilities may conflict with compatibility or environmental parameters. The purpose and need for major facility investments require clear background information. Providing detailed, transparent information is necessary for sound local discussion about future facility requirements.

- *Screening development alternatives.* Participation by community planners allows local land-use knowledge to be considered early in the planning process.

- *Preparing a financial plan for development.* The funding options for airport improvements are influenced by the FAA's policies for reinvestment of airport revenue streams. As in the case of facility requirements, detailed, transparent information and clear communication regarding the financial plan are necessary. The funding for capital improvements may compete with other local investments, which should be discussed and prioritized to avoid surprises or misallocations.

© iStockphoto.com / Anton Foltin

FORECASTING FUTURE AVIATION DEMAND

The community planner can be a vital participant in the preparation of aviation forecasts early in the airport master planning process by providing local knowledge and serving as a resource for socioeconomic factors in the airport's market area. The forecasting process is the first step toward envisioning potential futures for the airport, and it requires FAA approval of the activity levels it projects.

Aviation forecasting is considered by the FAA to be "the basis for effective decisions in airport planning . . . with any activity that could potentially create a facility-need . . . included in the forecast."[1] During the airport master plan process, the FAA suggests that the planners

- Prepare a reliable activity baseline

- Select an appropriate forecast methodology

- Develop a forecast

- Compare the projections to other forecasts for reasonableness

- Submit the forecasts to the FAA for approval[2]

The FAA asks that aviation forecasts be based on reasonable planning assumptions, use current data, and be developed using appropriate forecast methods. Accordingly, the FAA is one of several key stakeholders that should be engaged early in the airport planning process. It typically represents a broad national perspective for aviation forecasting. The FAA's approval of forecasts serves as a national basis for planning and funding decisions, environmental documents, and benefit-cost analyses.

The level of effort required to produce a planning forecast varies significantly from airport to airport. Considerable effort, including the use of elaborate forecasting tools and techniques, may be warranted in the case of more complex projects. An existing forecast, on the other hand, may be all that is required for simpler projects. For simpler airfield planning, for instance, the most important activities are driven by aircraft operations and the fleet mix, since these define the runway and taxiway requirements. Where forecasts are prepared for terminal facilities and the elements of the airport infrastructure that support that facility, however, passenger levels are particularly important, with some airports requiring more complex forecast elements, such as number of peak-hour operations and peak-hour passenger flows. In addition, if demand levels are likely to be particularly sensitive to one or more factors, the planner should estimate the impact of reasonable changes in the underlying assumptions about those factors. For example, if expected growth is highly dependent on the continued operation of a specific operator and there is a reasonable possibility that the operator will close or decrease activity, the planner should estimate how much that closing or reduction would change the predicted demand.

A number of forecasts are readily available for use in developing and evaluating the master plan forecast. These include the FAA Terminal Area Forecast (TAF), state aviation system plans, and other planning efforts. In fact, one of the key steps in the FAA's review and approval of the forecasts is comparing the projections with the TAF system, which makes up the official forecast of aviation activity at FAA facilities. The TAF, which is updated annually, includes forecasts for active airports in the National Plan of Integrated Airport Systems. Where the aviation forecast is not consistent with the TAF, differences must be resolved if the forecast is to be used in FAA decision making, including approval of development on the airport layout plan (which is part of the airport master plan), resolution of key environmental issues, noise compatibility planning, and initial financial decisions.

The components of the forecasting process include data collection for existing forecasts, aviation and socioeconomic data, significant issues or trends, and input from key stakeholders. Analytical tools should be selected based upon the situation, with trend analysis, market-share forecasting, econometric analysis, probability (risk) analysis, and choice analysis examined. (See sidebar.) The selection of the forecast method or final model may drive how forecast scenarios are defined. In addition, the airport role should be considered, such as whether the airport is a primary airport serving the region or part of a multi-airport region, or whether the airport is an origin-destination (O & D) airport or a connecting hub. Connecting passengers rarely leave the airside area of an airport, to avoid delays and inconvenience associated with re-entering through security checkpoints; however, a connecting passenger may have more time to shop and eat inside the airside area. Origin-destination passengers, on the other hand, require all airport facilities, including highway and rail-access systems, parking, rental cars, surface transportation (limos, taxis, and buses), ticketing, bag processing, and security clearances, but may have less time and demand for certain vendor amenities beyond the point of screening.

Community planners' insights may serve as the best source to identify relationships between socioeconomic data and future aviation activity levels. However, there is no certainty in forecasting models. Historical data may not fully reflect all the relevant factors that will influence demand in the future. In addition, independent forecasts of variables such as population and income are uncertain. Using multiple forecasts develops a growth range for potential futures and encourages flexible planning for the uncertainties of the future. Scenario-based and probabilistic forecasts may differ from projections in the TAF significantly enough that the FAA may not accept them. Airport planners should demonstrate with detailed explanations the likelihood of the forecasts if they vary more than 10 percent from the TAF during the short-term period. Where the master plan forecasts and TAF forecasts differ, the heavy involvement of community planners is key—first, to validate local acceptance for the assumptions behind probabilistic forecasts, and second, to assist with the generation of detailed data in support of the forecast findings.

FORECAST METHODS

There are several appropriate methodologies and techniques for forecasting aviation activity at a specific airport. The selection and application of appropriate methodologies and techniques requires professional judgment. A forecast effort may involve a number of different techniques. FAA Advisory Circular AC 150/5070-6B, *Airport Master Plans*, provides a detailed discussion of several forecasting techniques, the most common of which include the following:

Regression analysis. A statistical technique that ties aviation demand factors (dependent variables), such as enplanements, to economic measures (independent variables), such as population and income. Regression analysis should be restricted to relatively simple models with independent variables for which reliable forecasts are available.

Trend analysis and extrapolation. This method typically uses the historical pattern of an activity and projects this trend into the future. This approach is useful where unusual local conditions differentiate the study airport from other airports in the region.

Market share analysis or ratio analysis. This technique assumes a top-down relationship between national, regional, and local forecasts. Local forecasts are a market share (percentage) of regional forecasts, which are a market share (percentage) of national forecasts. Historical market shares are calculated and used as a basis for projecting future market shares. This type of forecast is useful when the activity to be forecast has a constant share of a larger aggregate forecast.

Smoothing. A statistical technique applied to historical data, giving greater weight to the latest trend and conditions at the airport; it can be effective in generating short-term forecasts.

KINDS OF CARRIERS

The best representation of the current airline industry structure is a business model definition, which contains three carrier groupings: network, low-cost, and regional.

Network airlines operate a significant portion of their flights using at least one hub where connections are made for flights on a spoke system. The primary U.S. network carriers are American, Delta, United, and US Airways.

Low-cost carriers operate under a generally recognized low-cost business model, which may include a single passenger class of service, standardized aircraft utilization, limited in-flight services, use of smaller and less expensive airports, and lower employee wages and benefits. Examples of U.S. low-cost carriers include Jet-Blue and Southwest airlines.

Regional airlines provide service from small cities and primarily use smaller jets. Regional carriers are also used to support larger network-carrier traffic between smaller airports and the network carriers' hub airports. Examples of U.S. regional airlines include American Eagle, Comair, Expressjet, Mesa, and Skywest airlines.

Source: U.S. Department of Transportation, Bureau of Transportation Statistics, www.bts.gov

The forecasting phase of the airport master plan creates a basis for the facility requirements and resulting airport development plans. Active participation by community planners provides buy-in to the findings and can be a harbinger of the need for improved facilities at the airport.

Comparing Local Aviation Forecasts with FAA Terminal Area Forecasts
Linda Perry

A comparison of the FAA Terminal Area Forecasts (TAF) and local aviation forecasts for an airport is about more than just the numbers. The TAF for an individual airport is based on a "top-down" methodology, and its primary use is for planning and budgeting national air-traffic-controller staffing levels. In contrast, local forecasts are typically developed using "bottom-up," data-driven methodologies based on local socioeconomic factors and aviation conditions—not unlike the kinds of analysis that local planners typically do for other aspects of their communities.

Airport planners can be obliged by the FAA to justify material differences with the TAF. While one objective of a comparison is to understand the percent variance between the TAF and local forecasts, a second objective is to understand the journey taken in preparing local forecasts and the key questions that were asked—and answered, data permitting—along the way. Some of these questions may include:

• What are the "moving parts" of the forecast? Is a specific component of demand, such as low-cost carrier service, driving the overall trend in passenger traffic? Are other components, such as network carrier service, decreasing and being replaced by regional airline service? How will changes in specific components affect facility requirements and overall planning?

• What path was taken to arrive at the forecasts? Was it a direct route, and can others, with clear directions, arrive at the same place?

• Has a road map been prepared that clearly compares and documents the differences between the TAF and the local forecasts?

• How do the local forecasts compare graphically with the TAF? Are the results reasonable and consistent with long-term historical trends?

• Does the local forecast vary significantly from the TAF? If so, why?

The moving parts. An aviation forecast is made up of numerous moving parts, many of which are unique to a specific airport and community. Aviation demand at Airport X in Community X may be driven by a high-tech economy with above-average incomes that support an above-average propensity for both business and leisure travel. As a result, a large share of airline service at Airport X is handled by network airlines because demand is sufficient to fill large-capacity aircraft with 150 seats or more. In contrast, Community Y, with a population base similar to that of Community X, has an economy dominated by agriculture, below-average incomes, and a below-average propensity to travel. Airline service at Airport Y consists largely of flights to connecting hubs on small-capacity aircraft with 70 seats or fewer.

A critical first step in the preparation of aviation forecasts is disaggregating aviation demand by type of activity (e.g., network or legacy carrier, regional affiliate, low-cost carrier). Many a forecast and the planning associated with it has gone astray because it did not consider the underlying components of activity and how they might change in the future. For example, consider an airport with an an average increase of 3 percent per year in the number of enplaned passengers over the last 20 years. A closer examination of the historical trend indicates that, during the last 10 years, the number of passengers enplaned on network airlines decreased while regional affiliate activity increased fivefold. Although the overall growth rate may be representative of a long-term future trend, the potential implications of the shift in the aircraft fleet are significant for planning airport facilities.

The road taken. The approach and assumptions used in developing local forecasts for an airport should be clear and transparent, including the methodology used to derive them, the sources of socioeconomic or other projections that may have a direct effect on them, and consideration of factors not represented in the historical data, such as changes in aircraft and other technology that may affect the cost of and propensity to travel in the future. It is important to note that no one approach may provide input on all of the key factors that affect aviation demand at an individual airport. For example, an econometric analysis could provide input on the relationships between the historical nature and volume of domestic originating passengers at a given airport and regional economic conditions, which would allow forecasters to extrapolate how future changes in the regional economy might influence travel demand, using independent projections of the key variables in a regression model. However, such an analysis might contain little to no input on such factors as

(1) the role of individual markets in airline scheduling and service decisions

(2) recent trends in the airline industry that have affected an airline's decisions in route planning and aircraft acquisition, and

(3) the development of low-cost carrier service at an airport.

Input on these factors is important to the development of reliable forecasts that can serve as the basis for planning efforts at an airport.

The road map. In the FAA guidelines, two templates are provided for a comparison of the TAF and local forecasts.[3] The forecasts are compared for total enplaned passengers, commercial aircraft operations (air carrier and air taxi), and total aircraft operations. The comparison is presented for the base year and forecast horizon years, which are equal to the base year plus one, five, 10, and 15 years. The preparation of these two FAA-recommended templates standardizes the comparison and provides a road map for understanding the variance between the TAF and local forecasts for an airport.

Graphic representation. A comparison of the TAF and local aviation forecasts for an airport would be incomplete without an illustration. Although not required in the FAA guidelines, a graph, such as the 2009 example shown in Figure 3.1, facilitates a comparison of the local forecasts with the TAF in the context of the long-term historical trends. In Figure 3.1, the local forecasts are shown to be within 10 percent of the TAF in five years (2014) and within 15 percent in 10 years (2019)—and therefore, according to guidelines, they are consistent with the TAF.

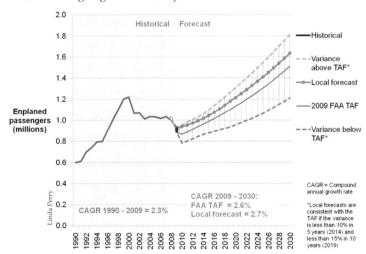

Figure 3.1. *Sample comparison of the FAA TAF forecast and local forecasts*

Variation between the TAF and local forecasts. In the end, a local forecast may differ by more than the variances outlined in the FAA guidelines on account of factors that can be supported and documented. For example, the base year for the TAF typically lags the data collected by airport operators by at least a year. During the course of that year, new airline service may be added and economic conditions may improve, both contributing to growth in aviation demand that exceeds the activity forecast in the TAF. Similarly, new airline service may have been publicly announced since the TAF was prepared, which will affect the forecasts and the planning to support that growth. On the other hand, a local forecast may be less than the TAF if a significant amount of airline service is lost due to an airline bankruptcy or a shift of service to a nearby competing airport.

PLANNING FACILITY REQUIREMENTS

Susan M. Schalk, AICP

To ensure a successful planning process, the FAA and the Airport Consultants Council encourage airport sponsors to "plan first; program second." This approach works step by step through the planning analysis to determine the facility requirements and needs based on FAA-approved forecasts. It then develops appropriate alternatives for airport development before sponsors select a preferred alternative to present in the Airport Layout Plan (ALP) set of drawings.[4] The primary point is that it is important to avoid "backing in" to development solutions. Accordingly, the following sections of this chapter survey the airport planning process, which moves from the forecasting process to facility requirements analysis and then, as a result, to consideration of various planned alternatives for meeting the facility improvement needs. Potential roles for community planners are also introduced in these sections.

Identifying Facility Requirements

Facility requirements reflect the unique circumstances of an airport and its community. One of the planning processes of interest to community planners is the analysis of aviation facility requirements based upon the forecast activity levels. The airport planner will typically begin the facility requirement process by comparing the existing airport facilities (identified during the inventory process) to the facility needs based upon the FAA-approved forecast demands.

The facility requirements analysis can be based upon the shortcomings or problems measured in terms of size, quantities, or best practices in areas such as safety, security, and capacity. To that end, the FAA has stated that the facility analysis needs to

> clearly define the aviation problems and why the airport needs to resolve them. Findings supporting a problem, and the potential solutions to that problem, must be clearly documented. Planners should ensure that this needs analysis provides information sufficient to provide a basis for describing the purpose and need for proposed Federal actions. Care should be taken that the facility requirements are not so narrowly defined that they point to a single solution.[5]

The community planner should note that facility requirements may not be as basic as whether a longer runway or new terminal building is needed. Sometimes requirements are driven by the desire for proactive safety improvements, using the best design practices. Such improvements could include better connecting taxiway layouts or runway signage intended to decrease potential runway incursions, which are defined as the unauthorized presence or crossings by aircraft, vehicles, or pedestrians in areas designated for the landing or takeoff of aircraft. The FAA has established that its foremost commitment is to safety, with the goals of achieving the lowest possible accident rate and constantly improving safety. The FAA is "moving away from the anecdotal approach to safety and instead using data-analysis to prevent accidents before they happen," through the implementation of Safety Management Systems (SMS) to collect and examine data in order to isolate trends.[6] For example, the number and types of runway incursions have been counted nationally, with proactive facility improvements partly driven by those findings. The implementation of SMS will affect facility planning as well. For example, the FAA's "Call to Action" to the industry regarding runway safety is resulting in measures to reduce runway incursions through changes in both facilities and technology. In short, facility investments that provide safety improvements have become the highest priority for funding of facility needs.[7]

In addition to considering shortfalls or problems when comparing existing facilities to demands, understanding the role of the airport in the region and the national system is important to facility analysis. The airport's role in the system needs to be integrated with the community's vision and strategy. Where the needs of the airport differ locally from the needs within the national system, the planning process needs to bring all stakeholders to the table to address these differences and develop solutions.

From a national perspective and according to the *2009–2013 FAA Flight Plan*, dealing with congestion and delays also remains a top priority, both in the air and on the ground. In addition to reconfiguring airplanes' routes and approaches to airports, the FAA has identified the need to preserve and improve airports—both commercial and general aviation—in order to prepare for the future and maintain America's leading role in aviation. The qualities that set the United States apart are the size and complexity of its infrastructure, its safety record, and its history of innovation and aviation leadership. Between 2000 and 2010, 16 new runways have opened at large commercial airports, and yet the capacity of the airport system continues to be stretched beyond its limits at certain airports and regions. For a community planner, it is critical to understand the regional and national role of the airport while also developing a strong knowledge about the relationship between demand and capacity at the airport.[8]

In addition to matching the existing facility demands with forecast facility demands, the FAA has identified the following areas as also influencing the needs for facility upgrades:

- Capacity shortfalls, which are commonly driven by growing demand.

- Enhanced security requirements mandated by the Transportation Security Administration, including the flexibility to respond to changes in threat levels.

- Updated standards developed and adopted by the FAA or other regulatory agencies to correct existing nonstandard conditions and eliminate existing modifications to standards. If there are approved modifications to standards, planners should review the reasoning that led to those adjustments. The facility requirements chapter should indicate if those deviations will persist or will be eliminated in the new master plan.

- The airport sponsor's strategic vision for the airport. Such needs are typically associated with a sponsor's strategic business plan, mission statement, or similar plans that will require modification of the airport. For example, the modernization program at O'Hare Airport in Chicago is the product of the mayor's vision for building a 21st-century airport at no cost to local or state taxpayers. The O'Hare Modernization Program is transforming its airfield from a system of intersecting runways into a modern parallel-runway configuration, to reduce flight delays and increase capacity.

• The outdated condition, arrangement, or functionality of existing facilities.[9]

From the community planner's perspective, the airport planning process will follow FAA guidance and may raise issues that are not locally driven. In fact, the FAA priorities may place some projects ahead of others that have higher levels of local support. Active participation by local stakeholders allows early discussions and understanding to occur. Communication among all stakeholders is needed to be sure that complex issues are clearly understood, and it increases the likelihood that a consensus for action can be reached.

Facility requirements will be identified through a local analysis process, with solutions that are embraced by the airport sponsor and local community; the actual timing and funding for facility improvements, however, must be "driven by the demand level, not a time frame or a specific year. Therefore, planners should identify what demand levels will trigger the need for the expansion or improvement of a specific facility."[10]

Although the facility requirements process may be very straightforward in some cases, the community involvement with and vision for the airport are also important and may drive the results during this process. The community planner's involvement is particularly central where decisions are being made in the community's interests, such as when responding to issues about surrounding land uses or congestion. As stated in the FAA's advisory circular:

> the airport sponsor may decide that it is in the community's best interest for the airport not to continue to grow to accommodate forecast activity, or to accommodate forecast activity only up to a point. In these cases, the master plan should document this decision and indicate the probable consequences of the decision (e.g., demand will be capped, the demand will go unmet, or the demand will be diverted to another airport).[11]

SCREENING DEVELOPMENT ALTERNATIVES

Following the forecasting and facility analysis processes, a third planning process that allows proactive participation by community planners is alternatives analysis. This phase of the airport master plan "brings together many different elements of the planning process to identify and evaluate alternatives for meeting the needs of airport users as well as the strategic vision of the airport sponsor."[12]

One of the initial steps of this analysis is to determine which functional activities (airside, defined as the portion of the airport that contains the facilities needed for the operation of aircraft; passenger terminal; cargo; or general aviation) require large contiguous land areas and should thus be studied first, and which elements have greater planning flexibility and can be studied as secondary elements. Once this step is completed, preliminary alternatives should be selected for the primary elements. Preliminary screening by element follows, mostly using subjective analysis, and should result in an intermediate list of the alternatives by element. The community planner's involvement during this phase provides an opportunity to introduce and consider specific details about areas beyond the boundaries of the airport as a part of the screening for development options.

The refinement of methods for alternatives analysis is a key place for community planners to introduce local values into the screening process. Four broad categories are used during the analysis process: operational performance, best planning tenets, environmental factors, and fiscal factors.[13] The community planner can provide input based upon local experiences

FACILITY REQUIREMENTS AND AN AIRPORT'S STRATEGIC PLANNING

Rick Busch

With the continuing uncertainties and changes in the commercial aviation industry, airport planning has become an integral component of the business-decision processes required to manage and develop airports. Airport planners are being asked to take a more definitive role in airports' strategic planning and in optimizing the use of existing facilities, analyzing risk, maintaining practical flexibilities and contingencies for future change, and meeting sustainability and customer service goals. Strategic planning can take a number of forms—from a formal, airport-defined, and documented strategy for the airport's long-range development to the more dynamic establishment and ongoing refinement of airport priorities and policies to guide planning and decision making. By its nature, a strategic plan in any form embodies flexibility and responsiveness, given the dynamic state of the business-oriented commercial aviation industry.

To do this, planners must consider management policies along with or as an alternative to facility development and expansion, necessitating a toolbox of enhanced analytical and graphical tools and technologies; an expanded understanding of operational, financial, environmental, and business planning; and the ability to identify emerging trends, recognize industry challenges, and define potential future scenarios. In addition to developing a basic knowledge of the planning, design, and construction processes, planners ultimately must be able to communicate the strategic aspects of airport planning and development to insure that agreed-upon planning objectives are met but that appropriate flexibility and contingencies are preserved.

The definition of facilities required to meet the growth forecast for an airport is a critical step in the planning process, as it establishes a baseline from which other constraints, conditions, demands, and opportunities are explored. In other words, the definition of facility requirements is an analytical beginning.

While the facility requirements form the basis for the subsequent development of concepts that undergird facilities that are to accommodate future demand, these requirements have traditionally been developed using industry planning standards and metrics, many of which evolved well before more recent operational, technological, and other advances were available. Consequently, the traditional approach to defining facility requirements has typically represented the most demanding development requirements.

More recently, airports have increasingly focused on a strategic approach to facility development and operation in an effort to reflect organization priorities, environmental sensitivities, fiscal discipline, stakeholder interests, and regulatory and other demands. Aligning the future facility development, projected as necessary to meet forecast demand, with this strategic approach to development provides an opportunity to define facility requirements to specifically reflect the airport's

priorities. For example, during the Denver International Airport master planning process, strategic planning was integrated with the development of facility requirements in a number of ways. Among them:

- Specific airport components were assessed under varying levels of common or joint use in order to explore the optimization and maximum potential use of existing facilities before an investment in additional facilities would be required.

- Coordination with airlines and other stakeholders was undertaken to understand what facility users envisioned as possibilities in the evolution of passenger and baggage-handling processes, equipment, and facilities.

- Investigations were made into potential roadway- and curbside-management options for protecting the operational flexibility and dynamic management of the curbside during peak or surged demand conditions, as an alternative to expanding the curbside in the near term.

- Potential expansion opportunities within existing facilities and leaseholds were explored, in order to predict when specific facility-development decisions are going to have to be made.

While the definition of facility requirements remains primarily a quantitatively based analytic effort, there are increasing opportunities to explore varying scenarios that not only map reasonable future development needs but also reflect an airport's broader, and sometimes evolving, strategic priorities and constraints. Linking facility requirements with airport strategic planning during the master planning process can support flexibility in future development, appropriately reflect industry evolution and uncertainties, and serve as a tangible demonstration of an airport's commitment to integrated and balanced planning and development.

Because planners must work with the FAA, airlines, and various stakeholders to successfully address issues and achieve consensus on future development at an airport, they are often the primary link among the airport, stakeholders, other airports in the region, and surrounding communities in terms of coordination and collaborative planning efforts for transportation, land-use compatibility, and economic development. By aligning the projected facility requirements with the airport's broader strategic and business objectives, planners can help an airport articulate its vision for the future. Stakeholder and community acceptance and support of long-range airport development is one objective of the planning process as is demonstrating a future that is based on not only a quantitative analysis of need but one that preserves flexibility and prioritizes solutions that balance physical, operational, and financial demands.

ALTERNATIVES ANALYSIS AND AN AIRPORT'S STRATEGIC PLANNING

John van Woensel

Airport directors are charged with charting and implementing the missions of their airports. Doing so involves periodic development of airport-wide comprehensive or master plans, as well as the development of an associated project-implementation strategy. Without such a strategy, a completed airport plan will not serve as the blueprint for future development it was intended to be and is no more than the product of an academic exercise.

The airport planning process addresses facilities that are needed to adequately meet expected future demand levels, a technical process that reflects a certain degree of stakeholder input. Airport strategy, on the other hand, considers the greater airport and regional context of the plan and its implementation, including adoption by the governing agency, and often involves negotiations with other organizations and interactions with politicians, airport neighbors, and regulators. A successful and implementable plan must fit with the overall strategy of the airport. The following examples illustrate the importance of the consideration of overall strategy during the planning process:

- At a large airport located in two different jurisdictions, a site for a new control tower was selected because it fell within the same political jurisdiction that owned the airport. The planning process, though, had focused on the best site from a purely aeronautical perspective and had not considered the important and ultimately deciding strategic need to have the tower-related jobs and taxes within the city boundary.

- At a large hub airport, the need for two more parallel runways over the 20-year planning period was clearly identified, based on projected strong future demand and already high existing air-traffic delay levels. In order to obtain needed approvals for implementing the planned first new runway, however, the airport director was forced to exclude the needed second new runway from the plan—not doing so might have induced lawsuits and other opposition. Although the first runway was built, some 15 years later the increasingly congested airport remains without an adopted long-term solution.

- In a reverse case at a small commercial-service airport in a rapidly growing part of the country, a new runway will not be needed until well after the 20-year planning period, but for strategic reasons it was deliberately included in the airport master plan. Doing so served to help limit future incompatible residential development nearby, reflecting the regional strategy of managed and sustainable growth.

Some strategic considerations fall outside the scope of work of the planners, but for their proposed projects to be implementable and therefore meaningful, the airport's planners must always consider overall airport strategy. At the same time, a plan must maintain a solid technical justification for proposed projects—particularly in the near term—or environmental and financial approvals will likely not be attainable.

in three of these four areas, while evaluating operational performance requires aviation expertise.

Among the fiscal factors, affordability can be a sticky question and should be considered early and openly in the planning process. It is common for the alternatives analysis process to include consideration of preliminary cost estimates as one of the screening measures that help rank the alternatives or to establish affordability parameters as a threshold requirement for further consideration.

At the conclusion of the alternatives analysis process, the airport sponsor selects the preferred alternative and documents the proposed improvements on a set of plans referred to as the Airport Layout Plan (ALP) drawing set. Like the aviation forecasts, the ALP also requires the FAA's approval before it will provide federal funding for the identified airport capital improvements. A community planner may not be as heavily involved in the specifics of the ALP; however, there are elements of the ALP drawing set that overlap with compatible land-use planning beyond the airport boundaries. (See Chapter 4.)

PREPARING THE FINANCIAL PLAN

Another community-planner area of interest in the airport planning process comes in the development of master plan financing. Financial considerations and local understanding tie in directly with the successful implementation of the long-term vision that the community has for the airport. From the FAA's perspective, the financial section of the airport master plan is to provide "guidance on what will be required to demonstrate the airport sponsor's ability to fund the projects in the master plan."[14]

The master plan should develop financial capacity information early in the planning process. By considering future airport plans in discrete modules (typically by facility), planners can consider the revenue potential of particular facility development goals. Incorporating strategies for revenue growth in the planning process increases the opportunities for finding financial resources that will make facility development more affordable. Airports look to commercial development strategies during land-use planning in order to find revenue streams. The planning measures include preparation of development scenarios, planning for the timing and extent of infrastructure improvements, and planning for phased build out.

The complexity of the financial analysis process is driven by the size and financial history of the airport. As one might expect, the financial planning at a large commercial-service airport is more complex than at a small general-aviation facility. In this context, community planners must be aware of the limitations that the FAA places on a community's use of revenue streams from the airport-generated activities. These policies restrict the use of airport revenue and require that airports that receive federal funding maintain a self-sustaining rate structure, with revenues from aviation activities required to be reinvested in the operation of the airport.

Regardless of airport size, the financial section of the airport master plan emphasizes the funding and phasing for implementation of near-term improvements, used to update the Airport Capital Improvement Plan (ACIP), described further below. The FAA states that "a more general discussion of the funding of the medium- and long-term projects is more appropriate [than a detailed financial analysis when the project is taking place in a short time period] because of the uncertainty of future funding and possible shifts in the importance of those projects."[15]

Typically, the financial section generates a three-to-five-year plan for the funding and implementation of the near-term improvements. The information delivered at the end of the master planning process is used to plan for implementation, to inform the community about upcoming investments, and to allow for integration of the airport improvements with other capital programs for transportation facilities. In addition to with the FAA, the capital plan should be shared with local, regional, and state organizations to allow for the coordination of capital programs.

There are a number of sources that typically finance major airport improvements, including federal and state grants, private funding or third-party development, passenger facility charges, customer facility charges, a variety of bonds, and local funds. Traditional airport projects—such as airfield, terminal, and landside (defined as the portion of the airport that provides the facilities necessary for the processing of passengers, cargo, freight, and ground transportation vehicles) programs—look to airport revenue bonds or Passenger Facility Charge (PFC)–backed bonds as a primary source of funding. Airfield improvements typically pursue FAA Airport Improvement Program entitlements and discretionary funds for a portion of the funding as well.[16] The percentage of funding provided by federal grants varies depending upon the size and type of airport, with larger commercial airports receiving a smaller percentage of grant funds as the capital source, reflecting the greater revenue sources available at larger airport facilities.

Individual ACIPs are submitted annually by airport sponsors to the FAA and are compiled into a national ACIP, used "as the primary planning tool for systematically identifying, prioritizing, and assigning funds to critical airport development and associated capital needs for the National Airspace System."[17] The national ACIP is formulated by the FAA in cooperation with states, planning agencies, and airport sponsors. It is a needs-based three-to-five-year plan of funding for airport planning and development projects. With the extensive demands for funds, the FAA must distribute funds to the regions in a way that ensures that, nationally, the highest-priority projects are being funded.

From a community planner's perspective, understanding the local role in the financing of capital investments is important, since local airport projects may be competing for funds with other community interests. A champion is needed for successful implementation of a major airport improvement program; this champion may or may not have emerged at the early point of community planner engagement. In any case, as the airport sponsor identifies the best funding sources, it must provide clear information about the purpose and need for improvements to bolster support. The community planner's input can strengthen the airport sponsor's communication plan by providing early observations and asking questions.

NONAVIATION DEVELOPMENT OF AIRPORT PROPERTY

Dave Rickerson

Airports with unused or underutilized property that may not be well suited for aviation-related development have increasingly considered developing nonaviation uses on the land to increase and diversify their revenue streams. The success of a collateral development program within an airport property boundary can set a precedent for the eventual expansion of development beyond the limits of the airport, with corresponding economic benefits to the community at large. Airport and community planners should and can work together to promote solutions that benefit their respective interests.

Some forms of collateral development can garner considerable support in the community, such as the solar-energy projects that have been undertaken at both Denver International Airport and Fresno Yosemite International Airport as a part of larger community sustainability programs. Denver's nationally recognized solar project is a two-megawatt facility that reduces the airport's carbon footprint by more than five million tons annually, while Fresno converted 9.5 acres of idle land to a solar farm that saves local taxpayers $11 million annually in city energy costs and reduces annual energy demand by an estimated 170,000 barrels of oil. Other, more traditional approaches—such as general commercial development, logistics facilities, and "just in time" office warehouse developments—are often viewed negatively by the development community, as it can seem as if the public sector is directly competing with private-sector development while having more favorable access to development incentives and infrastructure improvements and not facing equivalent tax liabilities on the land being developed.

There are a number of issues and nuances associated with the development of nonaviation land uses on airport property. First and foremost is the issue of competing with the private sector in the arena of general commercial and industrial development. There is competition to some degree, but in other respects the airport facilitates private-sector involvement through the myriads of third-party developments that are typically initiated in the wake of airport development. A further consideration is the overall value of the airport to the community at large and, in particular, to the business community within any given area.

(continued on page 36)

(continued from page 35)

The financial health, overall viability, ability to attract new service (by keeping costs under control), and capability of aviation facilities are all factors in attracting business and industry to a community. How many times has the term "economic engine" been used in a sentence describing a city's airport? Both the business community and the community as a whole have vested interests in the economic viability of the airport. Few communities will allocate direct subsidies to airport development and operations, arguing instead that the airport needs to be financially self-supporting. For airports that have land that is not required to meet aviation need, collateral development can be one way to expand and diversify the airport revenue stream and enhance financial self-sufficiency.

Planners face an array of challenges that must be overcome to support appropriate development. A well-coordinated and cooperative planning effort can be beneficial to the airport and its surrounding communities. Some initial challenges on the airport side arise from requirements set in place by the FAA through its Grant Assurances, Surplus Land Requirements, and specific requirements that come into play if property has been purchased under a noise-mitigation program. These factors and requirements necessitate the concurrence of the FAA prior to moving forward with a development program.

Just because there is property available on an airport does not mean it is viable for collateral development. There is an array of considerations in defining development viability—or at the least the best approach for developing—most of which are more familiar to land-use planners than to airport planners. These include:

- The availability of and ease and cost of providing essential utility infrastructure, along with a clear understanding of the ground access requirements of various uses considered for development.

- A definition of the existing site conditions and an assessment of the extent and nature of the site preparation and mitigation required.

- Demographic, development, and socioeconomic trends; planners should conduct a market assessment to understand business and industrial-base trends.

- The vicinity amenities or issues that either support or negate potential opportunities or specific development schemes and uses. For example:
  - High-end office development is unlikely in a high-crime area or in a community with declining housing stock, schools, or commercial areas
  - Are there supporting technical and educational institutions?

- The ease of access to major transportation corridors for movement of goods as well as access to alternative transportation modes for employees or customers.

- Are there initiatives under way to mitigate or alter the negative factors?

- The extent to which collateral development efforts link to local comprehensive plans and zoning, community redevelopment efforts, and adjacent community goals and objectives. Is it possible to tap into economic development plans and targets established by local, regional, or state entities? Can the development effort meet a key community goal that the community may not be able to meet on its own?

- The greater context of the airport. It is imperative to define how the airport effort links to the efforts of adjacent jurisdictions and the community as a whole and how to make the most of these linkages.

In the past, adjacent communities have perceived airports as adversaries. This often stemmed from the airport's impacts on the communities, not the least of which is noise. In recent years, relationships between communities and their airports have begun to change in some places. With recessions from 2000 through 2002 and much more severely beginning in 2008, there has been an increased focus on job retention and job development. In a number of cases, communities have supported job creation through collateral development on airport property, as the economic impact of those jobs accrue positive benefits to surrounding communities.

Finally, the success of a collateral development program within an airport property boundary can set a highly beneficial precedent supporting the expansion of the development scheme beyond the limits of the airport, again with corresponding benefits to the community at large. Some of the key challenges that planners need to consider and define strategies to address, relative to fostering on-airport collateral development, include:

- How to acknowledge but work productively with the limitations of municipal and jurisdictional boundaries on the planning process and coordination of development efforts.

- How to structure or extend eligibility for development incentives for infrastructure development to a nontaxpaying entity, such as an airport.

- How to develop appropriate flexible, perhaps performance-based, land-use and development controls for airport-related development.

- How to best define a cooperative collateral development process and implementation program for a municipality and an airport.

In addition to investments in airport facilities, important investments may also be needed to put successful revenue streams in place for the long-term financial support of the airport. This is another area where a community planner's perspective is critical because of the planner's understanding of other long-term financial investments in the surrounding communities.

ENDNOTES

1. Federal Aviation Administration (FAA), advisory circular 150/5070-6B, *Airport Master Plans*, July 29, 2005 (updated May 1, 2007); available at www.faa.gov/documentLibrary/media/advisory_circular/150-5070-6B/150_5070_6b_chg1.pdf.

2. Ibid.

3. FAA, *Forecasting Aviation Activity by Airport*, July 2001, available at www.faa.gov/data_research/aviation_data_statistics, and *Review and Approval of Aviation Forecasts*, June 2008; available at www.faa.gov/airports/planning_capacity.

4. Airport Consultants Council (ACC) and FAA, *Improving the Quality of Airport Projects: ACC/FAA Best Practices*, 2008; available at www.acconline.org/Content/NavigationMenu/Resources/ACCLibrary/ACC_FAA_Best_Practice_Final.July08.pdf.

5. FAA, advisory circular 150/5070-6B, *Airport Master Plans*.

6. FAA, *2009–2013 FAA Flight Plan*, 2008; available at www.faa.gov/about/plans_reports/media/flight_plan_2009-2013.pdf.

7. Ibid.

8. Ibid.

9. FAA, advisory circular 150/5070-6B, *Airport Master Plans*.

10. Ibid.

11. Ibid.

12. Ibid.

13. Ibid.

14. Ibid.

15. Ibid.

16. FAA, order 5100.38C, "Airport Improvement Program (AIP) Handbook," June 28, 2005; available at www.faa.gov/airports/resources/publications/orders/media/aip_5100_38c.pdf.

17. FAA, order 5100.39A, "Subj: Airports Capital Improvement Plan," August 22, 2000; available at www.faa.gov/airports/resources/publications/orders/media/AIP_5100_39A.pdf.

CHAPTER 4

Enhancing Airport Land-Use Compatibility in Airport Areas

Stephanie A. D. Ward, AICP

 Airport-compatible land uses are defined as those uses that can coexist with a nearby airport without either constraining the safe and efficient operation of the airport or exposing people living or working nearby to unacceptable levels of noise or hazards. Compatibility concerns include any airport impact that adversely affects the livability of surrounding communities, as well as any community characteristic that can adversely affect the viability of an airport.

While the definition of compatible land use may seem vague because it does not identify specific compatible land uses, it appears this way for a reason. To determine the compatibility of a specific land use, several variables need to be considered, including:

- Management of the land use
- Location of the land use relative to the airport and the approach areas
- Attributes of development
- Ancillary types of impacts associated with the land use

As discussed in Chapter 1, the intersection between airport planning and community planning occurs primarily around the issue of the compatibility of the airport's surrounding land uses. A recent Airport Comprehensive Research Program (ACRP) guide provided the findings of extensive research on land-use fundamentals, and those compatibility findings are summarized here.[1]

Land-use compatibility near airports is composed of two elements: the concerns associated with compatibility, and the type of land use considered. These elements combined help determine the level of compatibility a given land use has with its surrounding environs. While general types of land uses are typically considered to be compatible or incompatible, it is important to evaluate each use independently, since certain factors can cause what may usually be seen as compatible to be incompatible and vice versa.

The first element of land-use compatibility includes the types of compatibility concerns that affect the relationship between an airport and its surrounding communities. These concerns can generally be classified as related to either noise or safety.

NOISE

At times, noise is considered to be the key factor affecting or limiting airport operations, since it is the impact most often noticed by individuals living near an airport. Aircraft operations can create sound levels that produce annoyance in communities near airports, as well as affect speech, sleep, and classroom learning. These annoyances are of concern as they affect the quality of life for residents near an airport.

There are several factors that can affect the level of impact that aircraft noise can have at any given location near an airport. Some of these factors are:

- Number of aircraft operations
- Type of air service (commercial or general aviation)
- Types of aircraft (single-engine or jet)
- Airfield layout
- Location of the airport relative to surrounding development
- Time of day
- Percentage of time each runway or runway direction is used

Several other factors can determine a community's response to noise, including:

- Type of surrounding land uses (commercial, industrial, etc.) and noise levels they produce
- Types of surrounding environment (rural, suburban, or urban) and their ambient noise levels
- Configuration of surrounding land uses
- Noise sensitivity of surrounding land uses
- Past experience of the community with noise exposure

• Perceptions about the necessity of the noise

Challenges associated with noise-related issues stem from the difference between what FAA noise standards allow and what a given property owner may find or perceive to be an unacceptable level of aircraft noise. The FAA and the U.S. Department of Housing and Urban Development (HUD) have defined limits for noise impacts that are based upon specific exposure to noise levels. They use a unit of measurement called the Day-Night Level (DNL) to measure average aircraft noise levels. A DNL is a measurement of sound (in weighted decibels [dB(A)]) over a 24-hour period, taking into account quiet periods as well as times of aircraft overflight. A DNL of 65dB(A) or greater indicates a level of impact that can alter a person's quality of life. Unfortunately, property owners in proximity to an airport are still exposed to aircraft noise levels that they may perceive as an interruption to their daily lives. To better demonstrate a 65dB(A) DNL exposure, Figure 4.1 illustrates some common indoor and outdoor noise levels associated with particular activities.

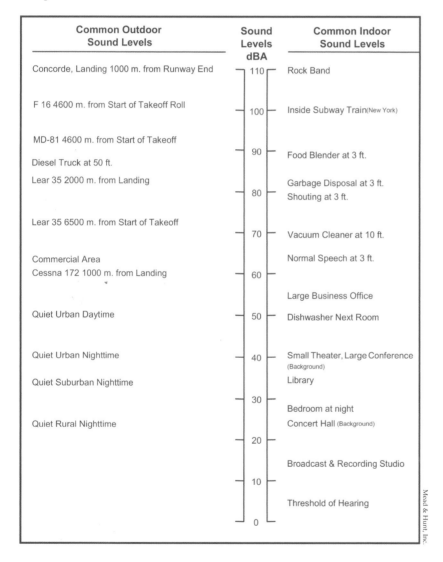

Figure 4.1. Comparison of common sound levels

The primary resource for federal guidance on noise-related issues is Title 14 of the Code of Federal Regulations, Part 150, referred to as Federal Aviation Regulations (FAR) Part 150, Airport Noise Compatibility Planning.[2] FAR Part 150 describes acceptable types of land uses for each DNL noise measurement. The basic approach to enhance noise compatibility is to minimize the extent to which noise disrupts other human activities or otherwise creates an annoyance. In general, the best approach is to allow fewer people to occupy areas subject to high noise impacts. When this approach is not practical, alternatives include:

- Shielding people from noise

- Increasing awareness of noise issues through educational programs

- Allowing land uses that have relatively high ambient noise levels or are otherwise not particularly noise sensitive.[3]

SAFETY

In addition to noise, another compatibility concern or airport impact that can adversely affect the livability of surrounding land is safety. Safety concerns are arguably tougher to address since they deal with what might happen, whereas noise concerns deal with what does happen. Maintaining the safety of aircraft and their occupants while in the air and on the ground, as well as the safety of persons on the ground near the airport, is vital. Safety concerns regarding land use can be divided into two broad categories: land-use characteristics that can be hazardous to airspace and overflight, and land-use characteristics that affect accident severity.

Land-use characteristics that can be hazardous to airspace and overflight include:

- tall structures

- visual obstructions and electronic interference

- wildlife and bird attractants.

Tall Structures

As described in Federal Aviation Regulations (FAR) Part 77, safety planners designate imaginary surfaces that identify the areas that need to be clear of obstacles or obstructions that penetrate the approach and departure paths for aircraft landing or taking off at airports, or that are in other areas close to the airport.[4] It is critical to prohibit tall structures within these imaginary surfaces. Low-level flight occurs on or near an airport during approach and departure, as well as during flights such as crop dusting and search-and-rescue operations. Collisions with tall structures during any stage of flight are obviously detrimental to the safety and welfare of those in the aircraft and those on the ground. Tall structures include buildings, objects, and natural vegetative growth, such as trees. Since they adversely affect approach corridors and instrument approach altitudes, tall objects such as multistory structures, power lines, wind farms, telecommunication towers, or tall trees should be discouraged near airport traffic patterns and flight paths.

The risk to aircraft safety associated with tall structures can be minimized if structures are clearly marked with lighting and if the airport issues a Notice to Airmen (NOTAM) to pilots. In order to evaluate proposed construction, the FAA has created a form (Form 7460-1) that is required for any proposed construction or alteration that is more than 200 feet above ground level at its site or that is of greater height than an imaginary surface at a slope of 100:1 for a horizontal distance of 20,000 feet from the nearest point of the nearest runway.[5] The FAA evaluates the forms based on the FAR Part 77 provisions, which require that an aeronautical study be conducted to determine whether or not a proposed construction project would pose a hazard to navigable airspace.

Visual Obstructions

Although they are not physical obstructions in the same sense that tall structures are, visual obstructions also pose hazards to flight by reducing a pilot's visibility. Many aircraft operations occur without navigational aids, and therefore clear visibility in the area surrounding the airport is vital. Land uses that obscure pilot visibility should be limited to ensure safe air navigation. Visibility can be obscured by dust, glare, light emissions, smoke, steam, and smog. Consequently, each of these should be managed, when feasible, to limit adverse impacts.

Dust and dust storms carry sand particles through the air that can create hazardous conditions due to severe reductions in visibility. When construction or farming activities occur within the vicinity of an airport, there is a risk that exposed earth materials will be carried by high winds across airport operational areas. Areas where low-level flight altitudes occur are susceptible to dust storms during approach and departure. Caution should be exercised to minimize earth disturbance and the creation of open dirt areas that can contribute to these issues.

Glare produced from reflective surfaces can blind or distract pilots during low-level flight altitudes. Water surfaces such as stormwater detention ponds and light-colored or mirrored building materials can produce glare as well. It is important to evaluate these items during site plan review and to consider whether or not they may affect a pilot's vision. Measures should be taken to minimize the use of reflective materials in proximity to the airport.

Light emissions of concern to aviation are often caused by lights that shine upward in a flight path. A pilot's ability to identify an airport during low-level flight altitudes can be hindered by emissions during evening hours, storm events, or conditions of reduced visibility, such as fog. Also, lights arranged in a linear pattern can be mistaken for airport lights denoting operational areas. Bright lights can be distracting and cause blurred or a momentary loss of vision for pilots as they pass from darkness into well-lit areas. For these reasons, efforts should be made to require downshielded lighting fixtures and minimize linear lighting patterns near the airport.

Smoke, steam, and smog can create hazardous hazes that contribute to reduced visibility for a pilot while operating an aircraft. Generation of these conditions by land uses such as manufacturing and ethanol plants or by utilities such as electrical generation sites and nuclear power plants can pose problems for pilots. Furthermore, thermal plumes created by these types of facilities can cause air turbulence that could be hazardous to aircraft, even though they are not visible to pilots. The location of these types of land uses relative to an airport's operational areas should be carefully considered.

LAPORTE, INDIANA: PURSUING MUTUALLY BENEFICIAL AGENDAS

Maria J. Muia

In airport planning, airports of all sizes strive to guide incompatible land uses away from the facility while encouraging compatible land uses near it. This is a monumental task, particularly in communities where city planners do not fully understand airports or what land uses might be considered incompatible with them. However, sometimes city efforts and airport efforts can support each other. In the case of LaPorte, Indiana, recent city environmental initiatives assisted in promoting compatible land uses around the airport (Figure 4.2).

Figure 4.2. The LaPorte, Indiana, airport

LaPorte is in northwest Indiana, and it has attracted people from Chicago on account of its parks and recreation, low cost of living, and intent to be a green community. Recently, the Indiana Department of Environmental Management (IDEM) designated LaPorte as a CLEAN (Comprehensive Local Environmental Action Network) community. Only 10 other communities in the state have received this designation. LaPorte's environmental program includes many of the common green initiatives like leaf recycling, reduction in fossil-fuel use, conservation of natural gas and electricity, and a green material-purchasing policy. But LaPorte has gone one step farther in protecting the natural environment: the city is one of the few striving to prevent light pollution, an effort that indirectly benefits the airport.

The city's code of ordinances includes a provision that forbids the artificial lighting of telecommunications towers, which indirectly helps protect the airport's approach and departure paths from encroachment that could reduce the facility's utility, especially during inclement weather. Federal Aviation Regulation (FAR) Part 77, Objects Affecting Navigable Airspace, defines airspace surfaces around an airport, sets obstruction standards for this airspace, and requires FAA notification for any structure proposed near it. FAR Part 77, however, stops short of preventing the penetration on any of these surfaces; it merely advises whether a structure would be considered a hazard or not. Any structure taller than 200 feet above ground level or that exceeds any obstruction standard contained in FAR Part 77 is normally required to be lighted. Therefore, the city's ordinance banning the lighting of telecommunications towers in theory prevents the construction of any telecommunications tower over 200 feet anywhere in the city; it also prevents the construction of shorter towers if they penetrate the Part 77 standards. So as a side effect of going green, the airport is being protected from one kind of incompatible land use.

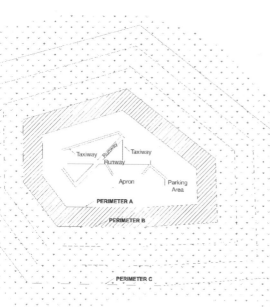

FAA Central Region Airports Division

Figure 4.3. *Separation distances within which hazardous wildlife attractants should be avoided, eliminated, or mitigated. Perimeter A: For airports serving piston-powered aircraft, hazardous wildlife attractants must be 5,000 feet from the nearest air-operations area. Perimeter B: For airports serving turbine-powered aircraft, hazardous wildlife attractants must be 10,000 feet from the nearest air-operations area. Perimeter C: A five-mile range to protect approach, departure, and circling airspaces.*

Maria J. Muia

Figure 4.4. *Airport fencing*

Wildlife

Another safety concern is the introduction of land uses near the airport that support or attract wildlife. Aircraft collisions with wildlife are threats to human health and safety. Between 1990 and 2005, wildlife strikes killed 194 people and destroyed 163 aircraft.[6] Since 1990, 82,057 wildlife strikes have been reported to the FAA; 97.5 percent involved birds, 2.1 percent involved terrestrial mammals, 0.3 percent involved bats, and 0.1 percent involved reptiles. The number of strikes reported annually has quadrupled since 1990, resulting from an increase in the number of aircraft operations, as well as increases in the populations of potentially hazardous wildlife species.

Monitoring wildlife activity and habitats on or near an airport is an important step in determining how to protect the airport and aircraft from wildlife hazards. Development and implementation of a wildlife management plan also play critical roles in airport planning and zoning by giving the airport the tools and techniques to properly maintain habitat management controls. An FAA advisory circular discusses various incompatible land uses and bird attractants.[7] (See Figure 4.3.) Guidelines urge airport sponsors to discourage the creation of pools, ponds, sewage lagoons, and fountains on or near an airport. Permanent water sources should be managed by removal, physical exclusion, or alteration of appearance. Successful retention/detention designs include temporary holding basins that drain within 24 hours and underground facilities such as French drains or buried rock fields. If drains and ditches cannot be removed, the banks should be mowed regularly to control bird nesting and perching there.

The management of potentially hazardous wildlife on or near an airport proves to be challenging because it typically combines active control measures, such as repellents, along with passive control measures, such as preventing and eliminating refuges and controlling attractants (Figure 4.4). Another key component to implementing these short-term and long-term control measures is to accurately monitor and record wildlife obstructions and control wildlife activity on and near airports. It is important to report all bird and wildlife strikes to the FAA to support the study of wildlife management. In addition to the wildlife advisory circular, the FAA has published a manual titled *Wildlife Hazard Management at Airports* to serve as a reference for wildlife issues within proximity to airports.[8]

Other Land-Use Characteristics with Implications for Safety

Additional land-use characteristics that affect accident severity are high concentrations of people and highly risk-sensitive uses. Available accident data suggest that the greatest percentage of aircraft accidents occur near runway ends during approach and departure. The risk of damage and personal injury to people both on the ground and in the aircraft can be reduced significantly by limiting the number of people in areas adjacent to an airport, particularly near runway ends.

Concentrations of people, or densities, are measured by the number of people per unit of area and are often categorized as high, medium, or low. Allowable densities around an airport can vary with the particular needs of the associated communities and the type of aircraft utilizing the airport. The degree of risk associated with density and the probability of aircraft accidents are generally based upon such variable factors as type of airport, number of operations, and type of surrounding land uses. Therefore, determining an appropriate density within the vicinity of an airport can be a challenge.

The following tools can be used in determining appropriate density levels near an airport:

- Analyzing parking requirements established in local zoning ordinances

- Setting maximum occupancy levels in accordance with building codes

- Measuring residential density in number of dwelling units per acre (du/ac)

- Measuring urban density and establishing an acceptable floor area ratio

- Surveying of similar uses

It is important to also take into consideration the frequency of use. A facility near an airport that is occupied occasionally and vacant otherwise may be allowed to have an intermittent concentration of people that is higher than would be permitted for a more frequently used facility. However, in general, the higher the concentration of people that a land use supports or attracts, the less compatible it will be near an airport. The lower the concentration of people, the more compatible the land use will be near an airport.

In addition to density, there are critical types of land use that pose high risks and should be avoided near the ends of runways, regardless of the number of people on the site. Chief among these uses are those in which the mobility of occupants is effectively limited, such as schools, hospitals, nursing homes, and so on. Other uses classified as critical community infrastructure—such as power plants, electrical substations, and public communications facilities—should also be avoided, as the damage or destruction of these could cause significant adverse effects on public health and welfare beyond the immediate vicinity of the facility. Furthermore, the aboveground storage of large quantities of materials that are hazardous—such as those that are flammable, explosive, corrosive, or toxic—should also be avoided, since they pose a high risk if involved in an aircraft accident.

A final characteristic that can affect the severity of an aircraft accident is openness. Open land generally has few occupants, thus limiting the number of people placed in harm's way; and open land areas can potentially enhance the survival prospects for the occupants of an aircraft forced to make an emergency landing away from a runway. If sufficiently large and clear of obstacles, open land areas can be valuable for light aircraft anywhere near an airport. For large and high-performance aircraft, however, open land has little value for emergency landing purposes and is most useful primarily where it is an extension of the clear areas immediately adjoining a runway.

Because open land areas must be relatively large (football-field-size or greater) even for small aircraft, planning for such areas must be made during preparation of community plans or plans for large developments. By the time a development has proceeded to the point where it is split into individual parcels, providing open land is seldom possible. Also, it is important to emphasize that "open land" differs from "open space." As the latter term is typically used in community planning, it may include wooded areas, sports parks, and other land uses that would not meet the purposes of open land. On the other hand, farm fields and even wide roadways may serve as open land but not appear as open space in local plans.

© iStockphoto.com/Jørgen Udvang

COMPATIBILITY OF DIFFERENT TYPES OF LAND USE

The second major element of land-use compatibility includes the type of land use considered. As part of the local planning effort, definitions of various land uses are developed to address specific needs. Since the specific classifications can vary by community, the definitions in this section have been kept broad to allow flexibility in interpretation and implementation by local planners and elected officials. Land-use classifications are separated into the following categories:

- Residential

- Commercial (shopping, business, or trade activities)

- Industrial and Manufacturing (industrial, manufacturing, and waste activities)

- Institutional (social and institutional activities)

- Infrastructure (special uses and infrastructure activities)

- Agricultural and Open Space (natural resource activities)

- Parks and Recreation (leisure activities)

The intent of this section is to provide a brief summary of the various types of land uses that may be found near an airport and the various concerns associated with seven primary areas of interest. This information is not meant to be a definitive list of specific land-use classifications that are considered to be compatible or incompatible with airport environs. Instead, it is designed to provide a general assessment tool to be used by elected officials, planning commissions, developers, and planners when evaluating the compatibility between a potential development and airport property.

Residential

As urban population continues to rise, residential land-use development often encroaches upon what was once open space surrounding airport property. Encroachment jeopardizes public safety and airport viability. An increase in the number of housing developments, bright streetlights, water detention ponds, and concentrations of people can be a detriment to aircraft and public safety. Residential developments near airports should be planned and designed carefully. Safety issues related to concentrations of people and potential noise impacts need to be evaluated when considering development of single- or multifamily housing and manufactured-housing parks.

Commercial

Commercial activities often require specific review and evaluation by local planners to determine compatibility with airport operational areas. Diverse compatibility issues arise between airport environs and commercial land uses, which can make it difficult to generalize the benefits or detriments created by certain land-use types. In general, smaller commercial developments are typically more compatible than larger ones. Strip malls offer smaller storefront locations and more specialized retail options that bring comparatively lower concentrations of people than larger retail malls do. However, both strip and retail commercial developments often have parking-lot light emissions that can affect a pilot's vision and also water-detention areas that can attract wildlife. More specifically, a restaurant attracts a higher concentration of people than does a convenience store. Additionally, patrons who use outdoor seating at a restaurant may be exposed to perceived noise impacts from aircraft approaching and departing the airport, which can make the area less viable or attractive. Local planners should carefully review the development of commercial activities in the areas near an airport so that concerns such as water detention, road alignments, wildlife attractants, lighting impacts, and building location do not create hazards.

Mixed use development offers commercial, leisure, and residential uses in a single area. Such developments can include mixed use buildings that incorporate retail or office space at the street level and living space on the upper levels, all within a central area. The combination of uses can create higher concentrations of people and may exacerbate the safety and noise risks of commercial and residential developments by combining them in a single location.

Industrial and Manufacturing

Industrial parks or areas designated to house industrial activities were historically home solely to industrial uses. Today, however, industrial parks are often a mix of industrial businesses, manufacturing facilities, office parks, and research and development complexes. Occasionally even hotels, restaurants, and retail activities have developed along the fringes of industrial parks to provide support facilities and stimulate economic development within these areas. Industrial and manufacturing land uses can include activities such as materials processing and assembly, lumber and wood product manufacturing, paper and allied product manufacturing, petroleum refining and related processing, primary metal manufacturing, product manufacturing, and storing of finished products. Each use has unique compatibility concerns, including the size of the facility, secondary uses, and height of the proposed development, each of which should be considered by the FAA and planners within the communities near an airport.

Industrial and manufacturing areas are typically encouraged within a community as a means to attract business, increase business tax-base and employment levels, and enhance economic benefits to the community. These areas are often located in proximity to major transportation arteries such as highways, interstates, railroads, and airports in order to provide intermodal connectivity. Transportation arteries are critical for companies to increase productivity and allow for just-in-time delivery options that are prevalent in the current economy.

Landfills and similar facilities such as composting areas, recycling centers, sanitary and water treatment facilities, and waste-sorting locations can act as wildlife attractants and require proper maintenance to avoid undesirable impacts. The FAA has provided guidance on how to comply with the federal code that restricts the construction or establishment of a municipal solid-waste landfill within six miles of a public airport that receives federal grants and primarily serves general-aviation aircraft and scheduled air-carrier operations using aircraft with fewer than 60 passenger seats.[9]

Institutional

Institutional land uses typically should not be located on or near an airport due to noise sensitivity and the risk associated with a concentration of people. Such land uses include but are not limited to places of worship, day care and elder care centers, hospitals, health care facilities, and educational facilities. These types of facilities may contain people who are unable to care for themselves, making evacuation difficult in the event of an aircraft accident. Institutional land uses can also contain large parking lots and water detention areas that can contribute to light-emission and wildlife-attractant concerns.

Infrastructure

Infrastructure facilities that are particularly relevant to aviation concerns include cellular-communication towers, water towers, and wind farms. General compatibility concerns are noted below; however, particular concerns should be assessed prior to construction within the vicinity of an airport.

The growing popularity of cellular communication has prompted the construction of an abundance of towers around the nation. Cellular-communication towers have appeared and continue to multiply in business parks, in industrial and shopping-mall areas, and along the national highway infrastructure. As a result, such towers have become a significant concern when evaluating height issues near airport environs. These towers can affect aircraft during low-level flight, approach, and departure.

Wind farms are becoming increasingly prevalent as the capture and use of renewable energy gain momentum in the United States. Wind farms generally contain numerous wind turbines that are typically very tall and cover a sizable area. Wind farms can also cause potentially hazardous conditions for air-traffic controllers if they create clutter on radar screens, which increases the difficulty of recognizing aircraft. However, a study conducted in June 2003 by the British Department of Trade and Industry determined that efforts can be implemented to reduce or eliminate wind-turbine clutter effects on air-traffic-control radar systems.[10] Additionally, wind-turbine blades can generate glare, which can create potential visual problems for a pilot. Many of the impacts associated with wind farms can be mitigated during the design phase of the facility, as long as the local community and developer are mindful of potential concerns and work to address them early.

Agricultural and Open Space

Agriculture and open-space land uses are typically considered compatible with airport operations because they have relatively low concentrations of people, limited concerns associated with visual obstructions or penetrations to navigable airspace, and limited impacts related to noise sensitivity. However, these uses are often wildlife attractants. Activities in such areas encompass an array of sites, such as agricultural fields (row crops, orchards, vineyards, farms), natural areas, tree farms, water bodies, and wetland areas.

© iStockphoto.com/Richard Klotz

The primary interest that aviation planning has in agriculture and open-space land uses lies in the impacts associated with wildlife and bird attractants. The proximity of farmland, especially row crops and orchards, to airports may abet detrimental interactions between wildlife and aircraft. If crops are highly attractive to birds or wildlife for their nutritive or nesting value, the risk increases.

The U.S. Department of Agriculture bulletin *Plants Attractive to Wildlife* provides a list of cultivated plants that can attract wildlife as a food source or as shelter.[11] For example, small mammals can be attracted to planted fields of row crops that provide cover. Large predatory birds are often attracted to these same areas because of the presence of the small mammals, birds, and rodents that hide in and feed on the crops and neighboring tall grasses. This can create a detrimental cycle of wildlife attractants that may lead to wildlife and bird strikes by approaching and departing aircraft. According to the bulletin, crops and vegetation that should be discouraged within the vicinity of airport environs include but are not limited to alfalfa, barley, corn, oats, rice, sorghum, wheat, vineyards, apples, and cherries. Best management practices can include reducing the amount of crops left in the field during harvest operations, selecting crops that are less attractive to wildlife as a food or shelter source, and notifying an airport when harvest or planting operations that may attract wildlife are to take place, so that the airport can alert pilots that wildlife may be in the area. Coordination of land-use concerns among an airport, surrounding municipalities, and local neighbors, such as farmers and horticulturists, is crucial to reduce the potential for wildlife strikes.

While the growth of agricultural products is generally discouraged in the vicinity of an airport, the FAA and many state agencies have acknowledged that agricultural uses are much more compatible with airport environs than all other uses. Nevertheless, if agricultural uses are to take place on or near an airport, there are certain dimensional standards that should be adhered to. The FAA has provided guidance on these standards.[12]

Open water bodies provide wildlife and birds with opportunities to drink, bathe, feed, roost, and seek protection from predators. A significant aviation concern with open water is its attractiveness to waterfowl such as geese. Coordination between an airport and local natural-resource agencies may result in the identification of specific species of wildlife, birds, and waterfowl that are hazards to the airport, as well as the development of a management plan for specific species indigenous to an airport's vicinity. Distinguishing characteristics of an airport and the associated wildlife in the area should be identified to address compatibility in a comprehensive manner.

Parks and Recreation

Parks and recreational land uses can generate a number of concerns vis-à-vis airport compatibility. Recreational activities can include sedentary activities, such as resting on a park bench or having a picnic, and more active pursuits such as fishing, swimming, hunting, and participating in sporting events.

In general, potential noise impacts, congregations of people, and wildlife attractants are the primary concerns for land uses in this category. Land uses that can create such concerns include but are not limited to racetracks, sports arenas, golf courses, casinos, traditional parks, sport parks, campgrounds, and playgrounds. These facilities often include large parking lots and extensive lighting and generate high concentrations of people and wildlife attractants, all of which are not compatible with airport uses.

Casinos represent another growing recreational land use. Casinos typically have large facilities that may accommodate a significant number of people. Moreover, casinos often have large parking lots as well as extensive lighting and large flashing billboards to announce events. Casinos may have restaurants that attract wildlife due to food in trash receptacles and litter in the parking lots, as well as roosting areas on rooftops and light poles.

Golf courses were previously considered to be an airport-compatible land use because of their large open spaces, low concentrations of people, and minimal lighting requirements. However, golf courses do have manicured lawns, trees, grasses, and water bodies that can attract birds, rodents, and wildlife to the area to feed, nest, rest, or roost. Consequently, golf courses are now determined to be an incompatible use.[13] The FAA has acknowledged that in some instances, airports have constructed golf courses on airport property prior to their determination as an incompatible use; such golf courses are allowed to remain. Golf is often used as a relaxing and meditative event, however, and when located on or near an airport the activity may be less enjoyable because of aircraft noise. In addition, due to the cleared open areas on a golf course, noise from aircraft operations has a tendency to carry for long distances, causing a quality-of-life issue for residents surrounding both the airport and the golf course.

More traditional parks and recreational activities such as camping and playgrounds also have quality-of-life impacts due to aircraft noise and hazards associated with aircraft accidents. Parks generally contain groups of people and attract wildlife due to litter on the ground. All parks and recreational land uses are discouraged within the vicinity of an airport.

COMPATIBLE LAND-USE PLANNING FOR AREAS ADJACENT TO AIRPORTS

Mark R. Johnson, AICP

As community planners know too well, once an area is committed to any given form of development, it can be nearly impossible to reverse the trend. Airports present serious challenges for their host communities when it comes to land-use planning. They require large tracts of land; they produce varied impacts beyond their boundaries; and they serve a dynamic and growing industry that often seems to be in constant transition. Furthermore, airports are important, if not vital, to local and regional economies.

Thus, local governments are faced with a demanding balancing act: to minimize the risk that future populations will be exposed to substantial airport-related impacts; to protect the long-term viability of the airport by ensuring that encroaching development does not choke the airport's long-term development needs; and to ensure that urban development permitted in the airport environs provides fair opportunities to property owners while producing lasting value to the community.

An especially difficult aspect of the airport/community planning interface relates to future airport facility requirements. New facilities can have profound effects on the surrounding environs. Construction of a new runway or the relocation of an airport passenger terminal, for example, can require substantial land acquisition, the rerouting of major highways and arterial streets, and the introduction of aircraft noise to new parts of the community. The inability to develop needed facilities can seriously compromise the ability of the airport to accommodate air-travel demand. In extreme cases, the choking off of airport development potential can lead to the abandonment and relocation of the airport—a project of daunting expense with potentially severe adverse impacts of its own.

If a local government is to establish a land-use planning and regulatory framework that promotes the orderly, long-term development of the airport, the airport must have a long-term master plan that defines the broad outlines of the ultimate airport development. Indeed, experience indicates that strong and visionary airport leadership is crucial to a successful airport land-use-compatibility planning program.

When the future of the airport is sufficiently well defined and broad in scope, local governments have the guidance they need to establish compatible land-use plans and regulations. That long-term vision also enables the airport and the local government to coordinate on future property acquisition and long-term infrastructure needs. Without a sufficiently comprehensive vision of long-term airport development, local land-use policies and regulations may be enacted that allow incompatible development in key areas, potentially foreclosing what could otherwise have been attractive long-term airport development options.

Many of the success stories in airport/community planning collaboration are at relatively new airports, developed since the late 1960s. Examples include Dallas–Fort Worth International Airport (1974), where Dallas, Denton, and Tarrant counties and several cities—including Arlington, Dallas, Euless, Fort Worth, Grapevine, and Irving—collaborated to form a joint airport zoning board; Denver International Airport (1995), where the city and county of Denver prepared the innovative Gateway Plan to promote a high-quality, sustainable community in the core of an airport influence area affecting Adams County, Aurora, and Commerce City, as well as Denver; Kansas City International Airport (1972), where Platte County and Kansas City, Missouri, have collaborated for years on a compatible land-use framework in the airport environs; Southwest Florida International Airport (1983), where Lee County has a system of noise overlay zoning, open-space and environmental protection zoning, and commercial-industrial zoning in the airport area; and Washington Dulles International Airport (1962), where Fairfax and Loudon counties, Virginia, are shepherding the emergence of an airport city, or aerotropolis, through implementation of a long-range comprehensive plan of highway, transit, and economic development–oriented land-use development.

Among older, long-established airports, Indianapolis International Airport offers an instructive example. The airport is a major air-cargo hub and consistently ranks among the top 50 airports in the nation in number of commercial passengers. Opened in 1931 in the farmlands

Figure 4.5. *Indianapolis International Airport, 1985. The passenger terminal is in the northeast quadrant of the crossing runways. Most of the area west and southwest of the airport is undeveloped and in agricultural use.*

Figure 4.6. *Indianapolis International Airport, 2008. Two parallel runways have replaced the original northeast-southwest runway. A new midfield passenger terminal has been built. (This photo was taken just before it opened.) Perhaps the most striking change is the intense development of industrial, warehousing, and distribution facilities west and south of the airport. The development was supported by new access to Interstate 70, immediately south of the airport.*

west of Indianapolis, the airport was a modest municipal airport for many years. Through the 1940s, 1950s, and 1960s, the city gradually grew to the eastern edge of the airport property. The burgeoning aviation industry and the advent of commercial jet aviation in the 1960s spurred the need for airport expansion. In 1975, the Indianapolis Airport Authority prepared an airport master plan with a bold, long-term vision. The plan called for the development of parallel runways capable of simultaneously accommodating aircraft on instrument approaches and the relocation of the passenger terminal to a midfield location. This airfield configuration would provide a high level of capacity and efficiency to meet air-traffic demand far into the future. Over the next 33 years, this vision was fully implemented. (See Figures 4.5 and 4.6.)

Bob Duncan, the Airport Authority's chief operating officer, credits this success to four factors:

- A consistent management approach and the consistent support of the Airport Authority's board of directors throughout the period.

- Strict zoning controls to protect airport approach airspace and to promote compatible land use in the airport environs, especially off the ends of the planned parallel runways.

- A comprehensive noise-compatibility program that established flight procedures to reduce noise exposure over the neighborhoods east of the airport. The program also provided for the mitigation of the effects of noise in seriously affected neighborhoods through sound insulation and acquisition and relocation projects.

- An extensive land-acquisition program that provided the Airport Authority with the land needed for future facilities far in advance of construction.

The crucial first step was the preparation of a visionary master plan. With this plan, the local governments (Indianapolis–Marion County and Hendricks County) had the critical information they needed to adopt airport-vicinity overlay zoning to protect the airport approaches. In the mid-1980s, the Airport Authority undertook its first Federal Aviation Regulation (FAR) Part 150 noise-compatibility study. The resulting noise-compatibility program proposed noise-abatement procedures that were quickly implemented and that were understood to be the model for procedures that would continue after the construction of the new runways. The noise-compatibility program also clarified the need for revisions in airport-compatible overlay zoning and set in motion several mitigation programs for dealing with noise-affected properties. This was all accomplished before the Airport Authority set out on its major airfield-development program.

Through these preparatory steps, the Airport Authority was able to enlist the cooperation of the local governments in compatible land-use planning while also assuring them and local residents that it was committed to being a good neighbor in addressing noise impacts. By the time the Airport Authority was preparing for its first major development project in the late 1980s—one of the planned parallel runways—the compatible land-use planning was in place to readily accommodate the development, even with the resulting change in noise-exposure patterns. Through good planning and the steady pursuit of its vision, the Airport Authority built the partnerships with the public and local governments that enabled it to move forward with substantial community support and negligible opposition.

CONCLUSION

Susan M. Schalk, AICP

Planning is a cyclical process that requires continual monitoring and updating in order to implement and maintain compatible land uses near airports. This process is necessary to continually evaluate and assess land-use concerns as they change and evolve within individual communities. Maintaining open lines of communication between airport planners and community planners helps protect both the airport and the surrounding community.

ENDNOTES

1. Stephanie A. D. Ward et al., *Enhancing Airport Land Use Compatibility,* Volume 1: *Land Use Fundamentals and Implementation Resources,* Airport Cooperative Research Program Report 27 (Washington, D.C.: Transportation Research Board, 2010); available at www.trb.org/Main/Blurbs/Enhancing_Airport_Land_Use_Compatibility_Volume_1_163344.aspx.

2. Title 14, Code of Federal Regulations, Part 150, Airport Noise Compatibility Planning, Final Rule, 69 Fed. Reg. 185 (September 24, 2004); available at www.faa.gov/airports/resources/publications/federal_register_notices/media/environmental_69fr57622.pdf.

3. See the materials prepared by the Federal Interagency Committee on Aviation Noise (FICAN); available at www.fican.org.

4. Federal Aviation Regulations, Part 77, Objections Affecting Navigable Airspace, March 1993; available at https://oeaaa.faa.gov/oeaaa/external/content/FAR_Part77.pdf.

5. This form is available at http://forms.faa.gov/forms/faa7460-1.pdf.

6. Edward C. Cleary et al., *Wildlife Strikes to Civil Aircraft in the United States 1990–2005,* FAA National Wildlife Strike Database serial report no. 12 (FAA and U.S. Department of Agriculture [USDA], June 2006); available at http://wildlife-mitigation.tc.faa.gov/wildlife/Resources.aspx.

7. Federal Aviation Administration (FAA), advisory circular 150/5200-33A, *Hazardous Wildlife Attractants on or near Airports,* May 1, 1997; available at http://rgl.faa.gov/Regula tory_and_Guidance_Library/rgAdvisoryCircular.nsf/0/53bdbf1c5aa1083986256c690074ebab/ $FILE/150-5200-33.pdf.

8. Edward C. Cleary and Richard A. Dolbeer, *Wildlife Hazard Management at Airports: A Manual for Airport Personnel,* 2d ed. (FAA and USDA, July 2005); available at http://wildlife-mitigation.tc.faa.gov/wildlife/wildlifemanagement.aspx.

9. See FAA, advisory circular 150/5200-34A, *Construction or Establishment of Landfills near Public Airports.* This advisory circular provides guidance to comply with 49 U.S. Code 44718(d) as amended by Section 503 of the Wendell H. Ford Aviation Investment and Reform Act for the 21st Century (AIR-21) Public Law No. 106-181 (April 5, 2000).

10. The study is cited in American Wind Energy Association, *Wind Turbines and Radar: An Informational Resource,* June 2, 2006; available at www.awea.org/pubs/factsheets/060602_Wind_Turbines_and _Radar_Fact_Sheet.pdf.

11. See also P. W. Lefebvre and D. F. Mott, *Reducing Bird/Aircraft Hazards at Airports through Control of Bird Nesting, Roosting, Perching, and Feeding,* Bird Damage Research Report 390 (Denver: U. S. Fish and Wildlife Service, Denver Wildlife Research Center, 1987).

12. FAA, advisory circular 150/5300-13, *Airport Design,* Change 11, Appendix 17, "Minimum Distances Between Certain Airport Features and Any On-Airport Agriculture Crops"; available at www.faa.gov/documentLibrary/media/Advisory_Circular/150_5300_13_chg11.pdf.

13. FAA, advisory circular 150/5200-33b, *Hazardous Wildlife Attractants on or near Airports*; available at http://wildlife-mitigation.tc.faa.gov/wildlife/downloads/150_5200_33b.pdf.

CHAPTER 5

The Environmental Phase and Other Steps
after the Airport Master Plan

Susan M. Schalk, AICP

Airport planners can be vital participants in driving what happens after an airport master plan is published. More important, community planners can work hand in hand with airport planners during the period between planning and implementation. This chapter provides information about activities that follow the publication of an airport master plan, sustainability trends, and more formal environmental-analysis processes.

ACTIVITIES THAT FOLLOW AIRPORT MASTER PLAN PUBLICATION

Once the airport master plan is published, what happens next may be driven by two factors: community acceptance and affordability. Community acceptance is critical because closing the distance between a planning concept and the reality of implementation often depends upon public will. Major improvements often require a champion. The sponsor and the FAA cannot conjure up that champion; however, the sponsor can bolster the justification for the improvements.

Justification for major airport improvements requires clear communication. In some cases, due to the complexity of the aviation needs, being transparent may not be enough. It is also especially important to address points of conflict or controversial questions. Acceptance by the community entails each of the following considerations:

• A sound communication plan is needed.

• Justification of the plan needs to become part of daily conversations.

• Participants should be carefully selected in the development of the communication plan.

• Components of the communication plan should be tailored with consideration for the audience.

There are four steps in developing a strong communication plan:

1. Identify the stakeholders. The stakeholders that participated in the airport master plan may be a good starting point, but it may also make sense to reach out beyond those participants now that the major improvement initiative has been identified.

2. Prepare a clear, consistent message for use throughout the communication plan.

3. Develop a list of the best tools for communication, with the targeted timing for the communication driving which of these tools should be used.

4. Assign the communication tasks.

The FAA actions that follow publication of the airport master plan culminate for the most part with the approval of the airport layout plan. As the community assesses its interest in implementation, the FAA may require:

• Benefit-cost analysis (for capacity projects with $5 million or more in discretionary funding)

• National Environmental Protection Act documentation (categorical exclusion, environmental assessment, or environmental impact statements)

• Safety risk-management document preparation

• Runway approach modifications (may require 18 to 24 months to bring all-weather navigational aid on line)

The size and complexity of the major improvement program should be expected to mandate the size of the communication plan or to drive further investigations about the critical nature of the airport improvement program. Simple investments may be needed to explore the next step beyond the planning process. For instance, it may be necessary for preliminary design work to occur in advance of further discussions with the community, to help streamline the process and ensure that all parties have the same understanding of the project. However, for larger visions to unfold, the development of a team approach may be necessary.

> A partnership with the airport operators, airport users, agencies, and local communities may be needed to develop action plans that provide planning solutions to ensure the best fit on local and regional levels. Each airport, each local community, each geographic region must play into the solution set, with the specific tool sets identified and implemented appropriately. What works at one location may not work at another for a variety of reasons.[1]

At commercial-service airports, the affordability question is typically measured by the airline cost per enplaned passenger (which should be reasonable in comparison with other airports). The range of cost per enplaned passenger can be very broad, from $4 to $10 per passenger to as high as $30 or more where major improvements have been made or where the number of passengers using the facilities is down. Because these are dollars-and-cents questions, developing financial capacity early in the planning process is critical. To address affordability questions with confidence may require further analysis of the project costs, with the development of project definitions or other means of moving beyond the airport master plan used to firm up the vision for the major improvement program.

The project magnitude will drive the need for and breadth of further project definition, which extends beyond the level of detail in an airport master-planning process. Project definition entails defining program requirements and establishing design criteria and guide specifications, using drawings, diagrams, and narratives. The project definition may include a project overview to summarize primary objectives and a detailed agenda for operations, maintenance, and administration of facilities, with complex descriptions to establish parameters for detailed cost estimates. In addition, preparation of an environmental management plan provides a mechanism to assure that best sustainability practices are in use during the development of a major airport investment.

Grand and broad transportation visions are currently providing a framework for the adoption of other promising planning practices. At the turn of the 21st century, the Federal Transportation Advisory Group developed *Vision 2050: An Integrated National Transportation System.*[2] That national transportation vision included the following long-term goals:

- An integrated national transportation system that can economically move anyone and anything, anywhere, anytime, and on time;

- A transportation system without fatalities and injuries; and

- A transportation system that is not dependent on foreign energy and is compatible with the environment (e.g., with respect to noxious emissions, greenhouse gases, and noise).

There are three airport planning trends that tie in closely with the long-term goals from *Vision 2050*: to incorporate safety risk-management panels in the airport master-planning process, to analyze the master plan using sustainability measures, and to present planning findings using the latest technological tools to collect and present data with geographic information systems. These three trends are also broadly incorporated in the community planning processes. In some ways, these systems (safety, environment, and geographic information) have been evolving on parallel tracks.

INTEGRATING SUSTAINABILITY INTO AIRPORT PLANNING

Carol Lurie, AICP

In airport planning, the use of sustainability practices trails the incorporation of best practices in community planning. In fact, the incorporation of sustainability in an airport master plan is a very new concept.

According to the Airports Council International–North America, airport sustainability is defined as "a holistic approach to managing an airport so as to ensure the integrity of the Economic viability, Operational efficiency, Natural resource conservation and Social responsibility (EONS) of the airport."[3] Internationally, airport operators have begun to implement sustainability practices and initiatives at their facilities. Motivated by regulatory mandates and environmental and community improvement goals, "airports are finding that sustainability makes good business sense."[4] The Sustainable Aviation Guidance Alliance (SAGA) reports that "airports that have adopted sustainable practices have found substantial benefits including reduced capital asset life cycle costs, reduced operating costs, better customer service and satisfaction, and enhanced relationships with their neighbors."[5] At U.S. airports, there are five main areas in which sustainability goals and considerations are being incorporated into the planning process:

- facility design and construction guidelines

- sustainability management systems

- sustainable master plans

- stand-alone sustainability plans

- capital improvement plans

Facility Design and Construction Guidelines

In 2003, the City of Chicago prepared a Sustainable Design Manual (SDM; Figure 5.1) in conjunction with the Chicago O'Hare Modernization Program to transform the airport's intersecting airfield layout into a more modern parallel configuration. The SDM guides all aspects of the massive construction project and is based loosely on the U.S. Green Building Council's Leadership in Environmental Energy Design (LEED) New Construction rating system. It includes guidelines for sustainable site management, water efficiency, energy and atmosphere considerations, materials and resources, indoor environmental quality, facility operations, and construction practices. Other airport operators followed suit in developing sustainable design guidelines, including the Port Authority of New York and New Jersey, Los Angeles World Airports (LAWA), and the Massachusetts Port Authority (Massport).

Sustainability Management Systems

Building on its design guidelines, LAWA developed the airport-wide Sustainability Performance Improvement Management System (SPIMS), which enables LAWA stakeholders to evaluate and integrate sustainable practices across the organization. (See www.lawa.org/uploadedFiles/ LAWA/pdf/Sustainability%20Plan%20%28Final%29.pdf.) The SPIMS process has six specific activities for integrating sustainability into LAWA's ongoing operations and is focused on more than new construction activities. The following steps are continuously reevaluated to ensure that LAWA stays on the leading edge of sustainability. The steps are based on solid planning principles of:

- Conducting a sustainability assessment of the status of LAWA's policies, procedures, programs, and initiatives; identifying those areas that could be made more sustainable; and encouraging more sustainable behavior and practices

- Establishing objectives and targets for achieving LAWA's sustainability

- Implementing initiatives identified by implementation teams

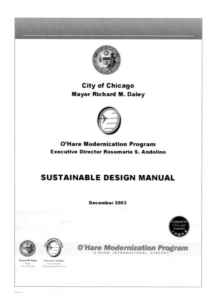

Figure 5.1

- Monitoring progress of existing programs, new initiatives, and projects that will help to achieve continuous improvement in sustainability performance

- Communicating progress through LAWA's website (and internal and external publications), to keep everyone aware of the sustainability activities performed at LAWA

The City of Albuquerque's Aviation Department has developed a sustainability management system that applies both to its large commercial-service airport, the Albuquerque International Sunport, and to the smaller general-aviation facility, the Double Eagle II Aviation Park.

Sustainable Master Plans

Several airports are integrating sustainability planning in the traditional airport master-planning process, either in stand-alone sustainability sections or by considering sustainability issues in each step of the process. Airport Futures is a collaborative effort between the City of Portland (Oregon), the Port of Portland, and the Portland-Vancouver metropolitan community to create an

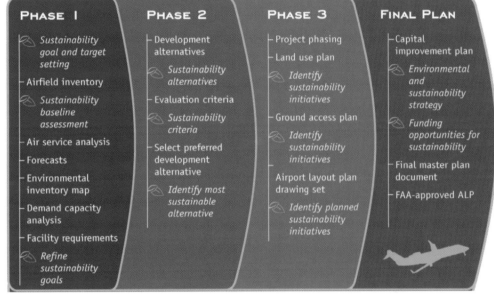

Figure 5.2. The Ithaca-Tompkins Airport Sustainable Master Plan Process

integrated long-range development plan for Portland International Airport. (See www.pdxairportfutures.com.) The port is updating the airport master plan with sustainability as its core consideration. The master plan identifies sustainability guiding principles that go beyond the typical subject matter of an airport master plan and addresses issues of generational fairness and the triple bottom line (measuring impacts on environment, economy, and society), community, economy, the balance of alternatives, use of resources, protection of natural resources, and accountability. Similarly, Tompkins County, New York, which contains the city of Ithaca, is preparing the first FAA-funded sustainable master plan, incorporating sustainability principles in each step of the process (Figure 5.2). During the airfield inventory phase, the airport conducted a sustainability baseline assessment and identified sustainability goals and targets. In developing alternatives, planners are evaluating them based on their ability to meet sustainability criteria and are also identifying airport sustainability projects to include on the airport layout plan. The master plan will conclude with a capital-improvement planning process that outlines an airport-wide sustainability strategy.

Stand-alone Sustainability Plans

Motivated by the requirements of its climate action plan, the City of San Francisco commissioned the *San Francisco International Airport 2007 Environmental Sustainability Report*, which documents progress in meeting the

TRANSITIONING FROM THE AIRPORT MASTER PLAN TO NATIONAL ENVIRONMENTAL PROTECTION ACT (NEPA) DOCUMENTATION

John van Woensel

The planning phase is the earliest one in the sequence of steps necessary to implement airport improvement or expansion projects. It is usually followed by required environmental approval under the terms of the National Environmental Protection Act, which spells out a process for when environmental approvals are needed and how to go about obtaining them. In the case of airport projects, the FAA takes the lead on environmental impact statements (EISs), whereas EISs done for the Federal Highway Administration are led by state departments of transportation. For environmental approvals and categorical exclusions, the airport leads the effort and the FAA issues the finding. Aviation projects are also unique in that many are subject to high levels of opposition and controversy. The transition from completed planning to NEPA compliance should be understood clearly by the planners, as this is a stage where delays are common and unexpected additional work is often needed.

It is during the planning phase that decision making occurs, addressing questions such as "Do we need an additional runway—and if so, where do we locate it?" "In which direction should we expand the crowded terminal?" or "Should we buy the adjacent farmland if it ever becomes available for sale?" Because of this focus on big infrastructure and policy decisions, detail in the planning phase is usually limited to just what is needed to support the decisions.

The subsequent NEPA phase, however, is different in approach in several key aspects:

- Significant detail is required to be able to environmentally assess and approve the proposed projects. This is especially true for airport projects where the FAA's NEPA process stirs controversy and opposition; a preliminary engineering design may need to be between 15 and 30 percent complete in order to support detailed noise, air quality, water quality, and other impact assessments.

- Under NEPA, the justification for a project must be ironclad, as it must be shown that proposed projects are "must have"s rather than "would like to have"s. In planning, on the other hand, "would like to have" projects are not uncommon, and projects may be adopted simply to reserve valuable airport property for future aviation uses, may be deliberately overestimated in size in order to be conservative, or may even be shown for strategic rather than technical planning reasons.

- The horizon of proposed projects differs between planning and NEPA procedures. The typical airport master plan considers a 20-year planning period, yet it is not possible to obtain environmental approvals for all the proposed projects. NEPA considers for approval only projects that are within the foreseeable future, usually five to 10 years out.

- Much of the time-sensitive information developed during planning is dated by the time NEPA assesses it. For example, master plan forecasts are developed early in the planning process, which usually last 18 to 24 months. Following the completion of planning, additional time is needed for subsequent funding and consultant procurement. It is therefore common that the adopted planning forecast is dated and requires updating to be reasonable for NEPA use.

It is important for planners to think outside their traditional silo and consider a smooth transition to the subsequent NEPA phase. While the challenge is to do so within the planning scope of work, the payoff for the airport is a transition into NEPA that avoids common delays and surprises. ◀

airport's sustainability goals and objectives (Figure 5.3).[6] Significant measures have been undertaken to reduce emissions, save energy, improve water quality, preserve natural

Figure 5.3

resources, and minimize waste at the airport. Key initiatives include 400Hz power and preconditioned air at many gates (which reduce air emissions), conversion of airport shuttles to run on biodiesel fuel, installation of solar panels, vegetation management by goats in sensitive habitats, and a solid-waste minimization and recycling program. The plan sets measurable performance targets and regularly reports on progress toward them. Similarly, for more than 20 years, Massport has prepared the Logan Airport Environmental Status and Planning Report (ESPR), which serves as the airport's master plan and annually reports on planning and development activities and the role of the airport in the New England region. (See www.massport .com/logan/airpo_envir_data .html.) Massport's progress in meeting its environmental goals, such as a high-occupancy-vehicle mode share and water-quality-enhancement targets, is shared with the affected communities and environmental agencies. The ESPRs provide baseline information for project-related environmental assessments and facilities' airport-wide sustainability planning.

Capital Improvement Plans

At the conclusion of the master planning process or in the annual capital-improvement planning efforts, airports are evaluating projects not only in terms of upfront planning, design, and construction costs but also in terms of their lifetime costs (also known as the total cost of ownership). Often when the operating costs of projects and initiatives are taken into account, the long-term environmental and financial benefits of initiatives such as recycling or so-called green construction become evident. In its airport strategic plan, Dallas–Fort Worth International Airport states its commitment to "the principle of sustainability, which requires a holistic view of the planning, design, construction, operation and maintenance of a facility so that decisions include an analysis of life-cycle costs, customer needs, and environmental impact."[7]

More details about how sustainability planning is being incorporated into administration, finance, design and construction, and operations of airports of all sizes and functions across the country are available at the website of the Sustainable Aviation Guidance Alliance (SAGA; www.airportsustainability.org). SAGA is a broad volunteer coalition of aviation interests formed in 2008 to assist airport operators of all sizes in planning, implementing, and maintaining sustainability programs. SAGA has consolidated existing guidelines and practices into a comprehensive, searchable online resource that can be tailored to the unique requirements of individual airports of all sizes and in different climates and regions in the United States.

ENVIRONMENTAL ANALYSIS

Susan M. Schalk, AICP

Typically, the airport master plan includes an environmental overview section, which provides a platform describing the airport environs for use during other planning phases or as background for further environmental studies. Where a major improvement program is proposed during the airport planning process, a thoughtful transition between the planning phase and the environmental analysis phase should occur. In some cases, where the need for detailed environmental analysis is identified in advance of the master planning process, an integrated planning process is used in order to enable simultaneous environmental analysis.

ENDNOTES

1. FAA, *2009–2013 FAA Flight Plan*, 2008; available at www.faa.gov/about/plans_reports/media/flight_plan_2009-2013.pdf.

2. Federal Transportation Advisory Group, *Vision 2050: An Integrated National Transportation System*; available at http://web.mit.edu/aeroastro/www/people/rjhans/docs/vision2050.pdf.

3. James M. Crites, "Airport Sustainability: A Holistic Approach to Effective Airport Management," Airports Council International–North America white paper; available at www.aci-na.org/static/entransit/Sustainability%20White%20Paper.pdf.

4. Sustainable Aviation Guidance Alliance, "Introduction to Sustainability," available at www.airportsustainability.org/introduction.

5. See www.airportsustainability.org/introduction/why.

6. Available at www.flysfo.com/web/export/sites/default/download/about/reports/pdf/ESReport.pdf.

7. See "Building a Future Together: DFW International Airport Strategic Plan"; available at www.dfwairport.com/dfwucm1prd/groups/public/documents/webasset/p1_008161.pdf.

CHAPTER 6

Conclusion

Susan M. Schalk, AICP

 Airport planners and community planners are encouraged to collaborate during the development of planning processes in order to weave the community vision, strategies, and values into the fabric of the airport master plan update. The quality of the coordination between airport planning and community planning is evident in the compatibility among the airport's surrounding land uses. This PAS Report promotes early involvement by community planners. As noted, additional land-use compatibility guidance is available from ACRP.[1]

Key to airport planning efforts is an extensive public-outreach process to consider community opinions during the articulation of goals relative to the airport and its future development. This report has also identified other opportunities for early engagement in the airport planning process by community planners, including:

• Participating as a critical stakeholder in the development of a vision for the airport's future, ensuring strong links between the community's economic strategy and the airport's long-term vision.

• Supporting preparation of aviation forecasts by providing local knowledge and research about socioeconomic factors in the airport's market area, with continued involvement in facility requirements, alternatives analysis, and financial strategies.

• Integrating compatible land-use planning that links the airport master plan with the comprehensive plan for the municipality or region.

The airport planner is often guided primarily by the FAA's interest in systematic airport planning that focuses on the airport's role in the national

Maurits Vink

system plan. The community planner's perspective, in contrast, will usually be driven by local conditions, which can be equally important to the success of an airport's master planning. Early partnerships and collective planning efforts are essential to assure that a sponsor stays true to the local vision for this asset while still meeting the FAA guidance for systematic planning. The best result will be that early engagement provides a sense of "ownership" for the sponsor and surrounding communities alike. Through collaboration with community planners, airport sponsors can successfully harvest unique, locally driven findings for their airport master plan update and, more important, foster community planner involvement that will increase the likelihood of adjacent compatible land uses.

ENDNOTES

1. Stephanie A. D. Ward et al., *Enhancing Airport Land Use Compatibility,* Volume 1: *Land Use Fundamentals and Implementation Resources.* Airport Cooperative Research Program Report 27 (Washington, D.C.: Transportation Research Board, 2010); available at www .trb.org/Main/Blurbs/Enhancing_Airport_Land_Use_Compatibility_Volume_1_163344 .aspx.

APA American Planning Association

Making Great Communities Happen

The American Planning Association provides leadership in the development of vital communities by advocating excellence in community planning, promoting education and citizen empowerment, and providing the tools and support necessary to effect positive change.

517. Community Indicators. Rhonda Phillips. December 2003. 46pp.

518/519. Ecological Riverfront Design. Betsy Otto, Kathleen McCormick, and Michael Leccese. March 2004. 177pp.

520. Urban Containment in the United States. Arthur C. Nelson and Casey J. Dawkins. March 2004. 130pp.

521/522. A Planners Dictionary. Edited by Michael Davidson and Fay Dolnick. April 2004. 460pp.

523/524. Crossroads, Hamlet, Village, Town (revised edition). Randall Arendt. April 2004. 142pp.

525. E-Government. Jennifer Evans–Cowley and Maria Manta Conroy. May 2004. 41pp.

526. Codifying New Urbanism. Congress for the New Urbanism. May 2004. 97pp.

527. Street Graphics and the Law. Daniel Mandelker with Andrew Bertucci and William Ewald. August 2004. 133pp.

528. Too Big, Boring, or Ugly: Planning and Design Tools to Combat Monotony, the Too-big House, and Teardowns. Lane Kendig. December 2004. 103pp.

529/530. Planning for Wildfires. James Schwab and Stuart Meck. February 2005. 126pp.

531. Planning for the Unexpected: Land-Use Development and Risk. Laurie Johnson, Laura Dwelley Samant, and Suzanne Frew. February 2005. 59pp.

532. Parking Cash Out. Donald C. Shoup. March 2005. 119pp.

533/534. Landslide Hazards and Planning. James C. Schwab, Paula L. Gori, and Sanjay Jeer, Project Editors. September 2005. 209pp.

535. The Four Supreme Court Land-Use Decisions of 2005: Separating Fact from Fiction. August 2005. 193pp.

536. Placemaking on a Budget: Improving Small Towns, Neighborhoods, and Downtowns Without Spending a Lot of Money. Al Zelinka and Susan Jackson Harden. December 2005. 133pp.

537. Meeting the Big Box Challenge: Planning, Design, and Regulatory Strategies. Jennifer Evans–Crowley. March 2006. 69pp.

538. Project Rating/Recognition Programs for Supporting Smart Growth Forms of Development. Douglas R. Porter and Matthew R. Cuddy. May 2006. 51pp.

539/540. Integrating Planning and Public Health: Tools and Strategies To Create Healthy Places. Marya Morris, General Editor. August 2006. 144pp.

541. An Economic Development Toolbox: Strategies and Methods. Terry Moore, Stuart Meck, and James Ebenhoh. October 2006. 80pp.

542. Planning Issues for On-site and Decentralized Wastewater Treatment. Wayne M. Feiden and Eric S. Winkler. November 2006. 61pp.

543/544. Planning Active Communities. Marya Morris, General Editor. December 2006. 116pp.

545. Planned Unit Developments. Daniel R. Mandelker. March 2007. 140pp.

546/547. The Land Use/Transportation Connection. Terry Moore and Paul Thorsnes, with Bruce Appleyard. June 2007. 440pp.

548. Zoning as a Barrier to Multifamily Housing Development. Garrett Knaap, Stuart Meck, Terry Moore, and Robert Parker. July 2007. 80pp.

549/550. Fair and Healthy Land Use: Environmental Justice and Planning. Craig Anthony Arnold. October 2007. 168pp.

551. From Recreation to Re-creation: New Directions in Parks and Open Space System Planning. Megan Lewis, General Editor. January 2008. 132pp.

552. Great Places in America: Great Streets and Neighborhoods, 2007 Designees. April 2008. 84pp.

553. Planners and the Census: Census 2010, ACS, Factfinder, and Understanding Growth. Christopher Williamson. July 2008. 132pp.

554. A Planners Guide to Community and Regional Food Planning: Transforming Food Environments, Facilitating Healthy Eating. Samina Raja, Branden Born, and Jessica Kozlowski Russell. August 2008. 112pp.

555. Planning the Urban Forest: Ecology, Economy, and Community Development. James C. Schwab, General Editor. January 2009. 160pp.

556. Smart Codes: Model Land-Development Regulations. Marya Morris, General Editor. April 2009. 260pp.

557. Transportation Infrastructure: The Challenges of Rebuilding America. Marlon G. Boarnet, Editor. July 2009. 128pp.

558. Planning for a New Energy and Climate Future. Scott Shuford, Suzanne Rynne, and Jan Mueller. February 2010. 160pp.

559. Complete Streets: Best Policy and Implementation Practices. Barbara McCann and Suzanne Rynne, Editors. March 2010. 144pp.

560. Hazard Mitigation: Integrating Best Practices into Planning. James C. Schwab, Editor. May 2010. 152 pp.

561. Fiscal Impact Analysis: Methodologies for Planners. L. Carson Bise II. September 2010. 68pp.

562. Planners and Planes: Airports and Land-Use Compatibility. Susan M. Schalk, with Stephanie A. D. Ward. November 2010. 72pp.

UCB